CW00376572

THE GRINGA IS MOVING TO PERU

Muffi Hiss

© 2018 Muffi Hiss
All rights reserved.

ISBN: 1983961981
ISBN 13: 9781983961984

This book is dedicated to Nicholas, to my mother and father, and to Peter

"All changes, even the most longed for, have their melancholy; for what we leave behind us is a part of ourselves; we must die to one life before we can enter another."

Anatole France

CHAPTERS

Acknowledgements	xi
First Trip To Peru	1
Meeting Giannina	9
Second Trip To Lima	14
Back In Lima	21
Peter Returns To London	25
Returned To London	28
The Flat Sold So Quickly	31
My Mother	38
Arrive In Peru	41
Nicky In Kinder In Lima	47
Back To The Fortune-Teller	49
Gloria Leaves To Vote	51
Decided To Buy A Flat	57
Bought A Flat - May 2000	59
Moving To The New Flat!	64
Trouble At School	69
Not Speaking The Language	72
Runoff Election – 28Th May 2000	75
Protest Against Swearing In Of Fujimori	79
13Th November 2000 - Gone To Brunei	82

Mom Arrives For A Visit   83
Spot Stolen   91
Looking For Spot   95
Spot's Birthday – 10Th August 2000   104
The Television Show   106
Getting Around Lima   112
Have Hair Done   114
Chocolate At School   117
Parrot   119
The Spanish Teacher And The Flood   123
School Flooded   125
Third Peruvian Election 3Rd June 2001   127
Mom Arrives Again   131
Giannina Mugged   136
Iguana   139
Lunch At Nasca   143
Children's Theatre   148
Suicide   151
The Bruja With Salvador   157
Hotel De La Borda   165
Nightclub Quique   168
Living In Peru   171
Nicky's Nanny In Lima.   173
Shopping   176
The Beggar   179
The Earthquake 2003   182
Nicky Wants To Run Away   185
Lecture   188
Nasca   190
Mancora   192
Cusco   199
Bullfight In Lima   210
Owl   219

Second Bullfight With Salvador   222
Huancayo   226
The Big Earthquake   237

ACKNOWLEDGEMENTS

To Giannina, without her kindness I never would have survived my first years in Lima.

My gratitude to Susan Harkavy who without her encouragement, and invaluable feedback, this book would have never been published. To Debbie Keeton who came to my rescue and sent the manuscript by computer to the publishers for me.

And to Juli H for all of her feedback. Thank you to George who introduced me to David Hornsby, who's editing got the book to flow. Also to Rafaella for designing the cover.

And to all of my friends who believed that one day I would finish the book.

To Nicky who was my inspiration to venture out way beyond my comfort zone.

Special thanks to Armandina and Irma, who were wonderful to us.

FIRST TRIP TO PERU

One dark and miserable London day I received a phone call from a friend, inviting us to use their house in Ancon for Christmas. Peter and I had plans to go to Florida, which we visited every year, but after getting an invitation to Peru I rebelled against another Florida vacation. Ever since I had known Peter we spent Christmas in Florida with my mother. Every year was the same, until our son Nicky was born, and after that I could no longer pretend to be excited about going to Florida. Gone were the romantic wine-fuelled dinners and sleeping in of our carefree bachelor days. Nicky was confused by the five hour time difference and woke every morning before dawn, which made Florida feel more like torture than a vacation.

Peter wasn't adventurous; his idea of fun was finding new restaurants and catching up on his backed-up pile of The Spectator. I held out little hope with him agreeing on Peru. But it became my obsession, and eventually Peter consented to spend Christmas in Ancon. Later he tried to discourage me, saying, "You'll be bored. There is nothing to do in Ancon except lie on the beach."

I first learned about Peru through a group of Peruvians I met studying in London. They often talked about Ancon; a small, once exclusive beach resort north of Lima where their families had summered for generations. When London became dark and dreary they fell back on memories of Ancon to keep their spirits up. I loved living in London and had no desire to return to my childhood home, but to them there was something magical about Peru, ingrained in their psyche. Young and rebellious as we were, they proclaimed an unabashed love and devotion for their families and their country.

London was the first city I had ever known. I was young, and a thrilling new world opened up. I discovered soirées, classical music, books; and was seduced by the easy confidence of older men. London opened my eyes to another life. It was a vibrant melting pot of people from every corner of the earth, it was 1970, the beginning of a new decade, freed from antiquated ideas and conventions, and there was a feeling of "anything goes".

The greatest compliment ever paid to me was during that time, by a friend of mine's grandmother. I was in my teens when we met. Every year she came to London to visit her family, and they brought her to call on us. In those days I was full of joie de vivre, with endless tales to tell, and because she enjoyed hearing about my adventures I exaggerated and embellished them beyond all recognition. In spite of my childish exuberance, she always conspired to sit next to me at lunch. Years after she died, I bumped into her daughter and she recounted that her mother had told her: "When I die I want to be reincarnated as Muffi." Her words cut like a knife. By then I was no longer the person who had inspired such a compliment, nor was I full of the joys of life, nor fun. The compliment affected me deeply – I had lost what was special about me.

Peter hired a driver to meet us at the airport in Lima. He dropped us next to the church in the main square in Ancon, which was as far as cars were allowed to enter. Ancon was established as a district in 1874, and originally people journeyed there from Lima by train. The town wasn't designed for cars, and there is no space between the rows of houses to accommodate roads. In the main square, we hired an Anconeta, which is similar to a rickshaw. It holds three adults across on a bench in front of the driver, who sits on a modified bicycle and peddles you to your destination.

The main square was swarming with people. Children scrambled through the crowd, dressed in light summer clothes and bathing suits, ready for the beach. Elderly couples sat on park benches, watching the world go by as their afternoon entertainment. There were vendors on every corner, some selling ice cream and others hawking homemade sweets, drinks, and things for the beach. Ancon was once a summer resort for Lima's elite, but during the land reform the government ordered several of its beaches opened to the public; which caused some of the elite to abandon Ancon for new developments that afforded more privacy and control.

The house in Ancon came with a cook and a maid, and Peter arranged a nanny for Nicky. This was one of the perks of going to Peru. I looked forward to our first holiday with Nicky where I could sleep late. Plus Peru is contra season; our Christmas is during their summer. And sometimes Florida was warm and sunny in December, but it could also be freezing cold.

When we arrived at the house, one of the maids was waiting to take our bags. She was short, sturdy, and smiled a genuine smile as she led us through the massive wrought-iron gates into a large atrium. The house looked Victorian; it was enormous and freshly painted, which made it stand out from the dilapidation around us. Ancon had seen better days, but there was something curiously majestic about her faded looks. Ancon's glory existed from another time; glimpses of her past shone through and would remain in evidence until the last mansion had crumbled and fallen to dust.

The bedrooms were upstairs. We followed the maid up an old wooden staircase that curved around the wall to the first floor, where it entered a gallery overlooking the centre of the house and then circled around to our rooms. Ours was the master bedroom, painted white, with high ceilings, and at the far end of the room were two sets of French doors that opened onto a large terrace. We had to look between two buildings to see the ocean, but that didn't spoil the charm, and I could hear the continuous sound of the waves.

Peter was just beginning to unpack when the maid knocked and came in to ask if there was anything we needed before she went to bed. I was headed for the bathroom to fill the tub, but when she saw the towel over my shoulder she remembered that the water supply to Ancon and to the house had already been cut off for the day. Regrettably she had forgotten to pump water into the holding tank on the roof, so we would have to wait until morning before we could flush the toilets and bathe.

Peter spoke fluent Spanish, so he did all the talking, but he was rarely forthcoming with any details and he got annoyed if I asked for translations. He said, "Hopefully we will have water by tomorrow. Don't complain. You were the one who wanted to come here. If we had gone to Florida we would be in our comfortable bedroom and bathed."

I didn't mind. I stood on the terrace alone, looking at the stars and breathing in the damp salty air, absorbing all the unfamiliar sounds and smells. Afterwards I climbed into the canopy bed and was lulled to sleep by the waves. This was where I wanted to be. Where the air was warm and fresh, where there were no cars, no mosquitoes; no need for air-conditioning, no supermarkets… and we had a maid to cook breakfast in the morning! What bliss.

Our house was only yards from the ocean. A wide promenade skirted the coast, and was crowded with people on bicycles, skating, walking and running. It ended at the furthest beach. We heard whistles distinguishing the different vendors, and the constant beep-beep from the horns of Anconetas warning pedestrians to get out of their way. Fishermen sat cross-legged on the beach with their families, some making repairs to their nets, others scraping and painting the hulls of old wooden fishing boats alongside the sunbathers. Vendors walked along the shore, hawking homemade confections and ice cream from old fashion trays strapped around their necks. Ancon was full of extremes: the very old, the very new, the very rich, and the very poor. Over time everything had managed to find its place. It was no longer the exclusive resort of the past, but many of the original families still kept houses there. There is something magical about Ancon. It has survived all the changes, and the people who love Ancon will always remain loyal.

After breakfast I persuaded Peter to take me to the local market to buy a Christmas tree. Ancon is surrounded by desert and there were no real trees available, so we had to make do with a tiny plastic one. If you searched hard enough, the market revealed its treasures. I found a stall selling trays of hand painted angels, trimmed with feathers, to hang on the tree. Then we found a nativity scene for the entrance hall, which we bought as the finishing touch. Everyone pitched in and helped, the decorations transformed the room, and we stood back and admired our work. But the following morning, when I looked again, I discovered the baby Jesus was missing from its cradle. We assumed Nicky had taken it. So I searched for it. I didn't want the maids to think that Nicky was being irreverent playing with the baby Jesus. I also worried that they were religious and would be upset when they realized he was missing.

Eventually I found the baby Jesus in a drawer and put him back in the manger. Incredibly by the next morning he was missing again. Nicky defended himself, insisting he hadn't taken it, but we had our suspicions. I didn't like to find the cradle empty. After several days of searching for the baby Jesus, one of the maids took Peter aside and told him that she was the one who kept putting him away. She said, "In Peru we place the baby Jesus in the cradle on Christmas Day, the day of his birth. He didn't exist before then. Could you please ask the Señora if she would leave him in the drawer, or to at least cover him until then," and thus began our first Peruvian tradition.

The largest tree in the main square was decorated with ribbons and boxes to look like an enormous Christmas tree, and Santa Claus arrived at the local church to give each one of the parish children a toy. For the poorer children, it might be their only gift, but there was an immense feeling of joy about the place. Ancon brought back childhood memories of Christmas: the anticipation, the excitement, the presents, and the spirit of everyone together. I had become indifferent to Christmas; dragging home expensive half-dead trees that shed, flashy decorations, and all the pressure to find the perfect gifts. Advertising started so early, hooking children on elusive toys and games that desperate parents combed the shops to find and were willing to battle other parents to get. Toys that would soon sell out, forcing parents to buy early to secure the coveted gift, hoping their children wouldn't be won over by another advertisement before Christmas. Happiness measured by the number of packages under the tree. After weeks of shopping, wrapping, and painstaking preparation, Christmas Day was anticlimactic. Nicky would rip open his mountain of presents, and afterwards he would look at the pile of toys scattered amongst the ribbons and wrapping paper and start playing with the empty boxes, feeling something was missing but not quite sure what it was. Christmas had become an enormous commercial nightmare that ended with the opening of the last gift.

Nicky loved Ancon. He spent most of his time there outside, whereas in London he was often forced inside because of the weather. He made friends with a young neighbour, and after that he always had someone to play with. But even with all their games of tag, hide and go seek, and chasing footballs, at the end of the day Nicky returned home as energetic and mischievous as ever.

When Nicky went too far he was put in time-out. Our bedroom doors were designed with clear glass panels to let the light through. He would stand on the other side of his door during his time-out, looking at me, and finding my frustration at seeing him hilarious. Eventually I found a maid's bedroom with a solid door that I could use when necessary. One day Nicky was caught throwing clothes off the balcony and I put him in time-out. He was furious, and I told him, "You are not coming out until you calm down, and I will not start counting your time until there is complete silence." It had always worked before. Time-out would distract him and he would calm down straightaway, but this time was different. Nicky wouldn't quiet down. His shouts resounded around the house through the vast atrium, winding their way into the kitchen, while I stood outside his door and waited.

After he quieted down and his three minutes were up I told him: "Okay you can come out." When there was no response I panicked and threw open the door, and there, sitting in the lap of one of the maids, was Nicky. She had heard him shouting and knew he was in time-out. She had put up the maintenance ladder that was kept outside in the service passageway, and came up and in through the bedroom window to be with him. The cook was also there. She was halfway in the window, but because she was somewhat older and larger she hadn't made it all the way in. I caught her standing on the ladder with one leg inside the bedroom and one leg out! Both of them were embarrassed to see me, but they thought time-out was barbaric when a quick smack on the hand or leg was punishment enough. They told me: "He is a little boy," which they felt explained everything. None of us said a word, but I was grateful to see their kindness toward Nicky. I was also thankful to have people around me who found tolerance and parenting more natural to their disposition than I did.

My mother arrived on Boxing Day. She was used to spending the holiday with us, so after having Christmas with my brothers, she joined us in Peru. Ancon reminded both of us of Florida in the fifties, when we had live-in help, when life was easy and we didn't have to worry about the endless drudgery of shopping for food, cooking, and cleaning up. My mother and I don't have a talent with language. At breakfast my mother would greet the maids in her dodgy schoolgirl French exclaiming, "Il fait froid!" – "It is cold." Those were the only foreign words she could remember. She and I were so different in many ways. I was like my father in the sense that I couldn't bear sounding foolish. I often remained silent, afraid to get the words and tense wrong in Spanish, whereas she wasn't embarrassed to use a senseless phrase in the wrong language. It was her effort to communicate. They were foreign words to her, and that was good enough. The maids quickly warmed to my mother, who smiled freely and towered above them. She often poked her head in the kitchen after breakfast, curious to see what they were up to, checking they had everything they needed, especially mangoes, and to see what they were preparing for lunch. Her lack of Spanish didn't intimidate her in the slightest; she didn't retreat into a shell of silence like me. She would enter the kitchen and point if she were curious about something.

Despite having people in the kitchen cooking for us, Peter often took us to Lima for lunch. He had spent his youth in English boarding schools and was unaccustomed to the relative tranquillity of eating at home. He felt more at ease surrounded by people in noisy, popular restaurants. We drank Pisco Sours, a mixture of clear brandy, fresh lemons, egg whites, sugar, and a dash of Angostura bitters. Which are high in alcohol and served before meals. I had been warned many times, "If you are alone, never accept a Pisco Sour from a stranger or you may wake up with him. They are stronger than you think."

MEETING GIANNINA

Ancon has evolved around a natural harbour, one of the best-sheltered anchorages along the coast. Its sandy beaches and protected cove make it perfect for bathing. The Humboldt Current flowing up from Chile creates one of the richest marine ecosystems in the world. Feeding the large populations of pelicans, sea lions, cormorants, and blue-footed boobies who thrive on the islands off shore.

Weaving our way home, through the masses heading to the beach, we heard someone calling our names. It came as a complete surprise, as we didn't know anyone in Ancon, and we looked over and saw a tanned exuberant blond, hand-in-hand with a child, waving enthusiastically and coming in our direction. She seemed to know us. We stood staring as they approached, not sure what to do. I was embarrassed, wondering if perhaps I knew her but couldn't remember, or if she had mistaken us for someone else. She rushed forward and kissed each of us as if greeting long lost friends. Only then did she introduce herself and her daughter, explaining that she was Giannina, a friend of our hosts. She was told we were coming to Ancon and had expected us to get in touch, but we hadn't. Peter and I had promised each other no social engagements while we were away.

We were easy to spot in the crowd. We were the only tourists there. My mother and I shaded by voluminous hats and long sleeves, our shiny sun-blocked faces mirroring each other's reflections as we made our way through the sun worshippers arriving for the beach. Peter's plump white body wore his sunburn like a banner that screamed, "I burn for England," which made us all the more conspicuous.

When I met Giannina I regretted that we hadn't been in touch, and we invited them back for lunch. Her daughter, also Giannina, didn't speak English, but there was no awkward silence. She chatted away in Spanish and held my hand as she balanced along the top of the curb as we headed home. After that we saw them whenever they came up from Lima.

Peter and I quickly settled into a routine. In the morning we took Nicky to the club, which had a roped-in area for swimming. Peter and Nicky waded into the ocean up to their knees, at times getting hit and drenched by waves. I watched them from the beach. The water was too cold for me, even to get my feet wet. We seemed to be the only ones awake at that hour and were the only people at the club, except for the maintenance men who arrived early and spread out across the beach with rakes, clearing it of seaweed and debris. The rest of the members slept late and surfaced just in time for lunch.

After breakfast Peter read the newspaper while Nicky played next to him. I stayed upstairs and read. One morning Nicky started screaming. I ran to the railing and looked down, and saw him standing next to Peter. He appeared to be alright, but he kept screaming, something which he had never done. Peter looked desperate. He told me Nicky had bumped into the lamp or the table, but not hard enough to hurt him. His screaming didn't let up, and then he doubled over, contorting himself as if in great agony.

Neither of us knew what was wrong, or what to do, so Peter reached over pretending to smack the lamp for hurting Nicky, but just as he gave it a little spank Peter let out a high pitched shriek and started jumping around, waving his hands in the air like a person possessed. As I reached the bottom of the stairs, Nicky stopped crying. He seemed confused, unsure of what was going on, and then he clapped his hands and begged: "Papi, do that again."

After Peter recovered from the shock, he unplugged the lamp and called in the maids. He showed them that the plastic protection had worn away from the cord, and that it was touching the metal base. The lamp was potentially lethal. The 220-volt shock could have electrocuted them both. Peter put the lamp away in the cupboard, but it was a losing battle because by the next day it was back in its usual place. Every time we went out they put it back. Defying all logic, the maids were used to it being there and didn't see it as a threat.

Peru was such a contrast to England, whose excessive health and safety regulations had taken over from common sense. Being in Ancon, with its absence of stultifying rules, was liberating, and I began to feel a sense of freedom and normality I hadn't felt in years.

Next trip to South America

We had planned to return to Peru again the following Christmas, but instead we got an invitation to stay with friends in Santiago and Peter accepted. Peter was born in Chile, he was a third generation Chilean, although half Bostonian through his mother. His family land and businesses were expropriated under President Allende in 1972; England then became their home. Peter was excited about the trip, he wanted to show us Chile and introduce me to his friends. We had also been invited to go fly-fishing off a private island in the south.

Peter's grandfather left a comfortable life in Holland for Patagonia, South America, where he pioneered whaling and introduced

11

Corriedale sheep, hardy and well suited for wool in tough conditions. He founded the estancia there in the 1880s. Peter's father eventually took over, and devoted much of his life to running it and building it up. He was in failing health when the expropriation papers were presented; living in self-imposed exile in England. He was too ill to fight. He signed the papers under duress, believing that the problems in Chile wouldn't be resolved in his lifetime; that it would be better to accept the little on offer rather than lose everything. He signed over nearly half a million acres, including all the cattle and sheep, for nominal compensation. Allende's Unidad Popular government ruled from 1970 until the coup in September 1973. Rio Verde wasn't expropriated until 1972, but because the papers had been signed Peter's family had no recourse to get the land back when Pinochet came to power a year later. The local community has since put up a memorial to honour his grandfather. This was hardly reparation.

I had been to Santiago years before, on my way to Antarctica, and I didn't like it. It was too far, there was too much traffic and pollution, and I disliked the food. There was too much traffic and pollution, and I didn't like the food. A meteorological phenomenon occurs there during the summer. Thermal inversion forms when a layer of warm air settles over cold air, trapping smog and pollution close to the ground, in the air you breathe.

After staying in Santiago, we flew south to go trout fishing with friends, on an island in Lake Yelcho. An employee collected us from the airport and on the way to the lake he stopped at a village to pick up last minute supplies. Afterwards we drove through miles of forest, and I saw, hidden amongst the trees, a house built from the fuselage of a crashed plane. When we reached the lake, a small boat was waiting to take us to the island. Snow-capped mountains broke the skyline, their glaciers firing off vivid reflections as they caught the sun. The driver helped us into the boat with our luggage, and then loaded the supplies. The water was clear and cold. Tiny fish darted in and out of the sea grass; feeding on the plankton we had stirred up as we pushed the boat out to deeper water before starting the engine.

When we arrived on the island, I was eager to drop my bags and go fishing while there was still light. But before I could get out the door, one of the staff reminded me that the fish we caught had to be released. We weren't allowed to eat them, which was a huge disappointment. I had envisioned a Robinson Crusoe existence of catching fish and grilling them under the stars, over an open fire. I was there to satisfy some primitive longing for nature. So, I despaired. We had come all this way, only to find more rules and restrictions. The unspoiled setting was reserved for the privileged few, and everything was meticulously controlled to keep it that way. It didn't feel natural to me. It also didn't make sense to catch a fish, release it, and then send an employee back to the mainland to buy one for supper.

Peter wasn't proficient at fly-fishing, nor was I, but I was less dangerous. He brought new meaning to safety glasses and protective clothing. We were using large flies resembling dragonflies, which were heavy and hard to control. After getting whipped one too many times by Peter's poorly aimed casting, once on my lip, our guide had to intervene as I dove at Peter and tried to throw him from the boat.

Nicky stayed on the island with a local girl, who we had hired to look after him while we were out in the boat. The island covered about two hundred acres, and just behind the house was an orchard, a kitchen garden, and marked trails leading up to a lookout point where, if lucky, you could see deer swimming over from the mainland. Fishing was the highlight, but I wasn't sad when the trip was over. I was ready to go back to London. Chile felt like it had more rules and regulations than Switzerland. At the end of the trip, Peter asked Nicky what he thought of Chile. Nicky told him: "Papi, you can stay in Chile if you love it so much, but I'm going back to Peru with Mummy."

SECOND TRIP TO LIMA

Our next trip to Peru was in July 1998. This time we rented an apartment in Lima, which Giannina found for us. When summer is over in Peru everything shuts down at the beach and weekends are then spent in the mountains, where it's less humid and sunny. The apartment we rented was near Giannina's house, and within walking distance of a nursery school, where Nicky would meet other children, and could play and make friends.

The first thing I wanted to do was to drive to Tarma, a village high in the Andes. Tarma is nothing out of the ordinary, but the trip up has spectacular views and climbs to almost sixteen thousand feet, making it one of the highest paved roads in the world. Peter hired a driver and we left early to avoid traffic and to give us extra time in case something went wrong with the car. We climbed up through the grey damp overcast Lima to another climate of clear blue skies. There were glaciers on the distant mountains and lakes surrounded by vast open space. After driving for hours, we realized that this trip was going to take us longer than we planned. The actual distance on the map to Tarma was short, but the steep and twisting roads made the journey much slower than we had expected. The higher we climbed the more hazardous the roads became. As we neared the highest point, the guardrails all but disappeared. The only thing between us and going over the edge on some of the tighter turns were the solid concrete shrines, built there by family and friends, marking the spot where loved ones had indeed plunged to their deaths.

I was sitting next to the driver. At times he would speed around the steeper turns, claiming it put less strain on the engine. He spoke very little English, so every once in a while I would prod him with my guidebook and make motions with my hand for him to slow down. After a short time he would pick up speed again and I would have to remind him again. Morbid fears and visions of dying flashed through my head - I thought of Nicky in his sweet innocence solemnly waiting for us with the maid, inevitably losing patience, excited, expecting that at any moment we would walk through the door; but us never coming home.

Some of the hairpin curves had so many concrete shrines built to commemorate the dead that they formed a protective barrier saving others from a similar fate, which was a blessing. It was hard to tell if they signified the most dangerous curves, or if it was because cars and busses packed full of screaming people had simply gone over the edge. Luckily there was hardly any other traffic, except for a few trucks. I became more and more nervous, and kept a sharp eye on the road. Out of nowhere I saw a car coming toward us, but it was still far away. I could tell that the car was going fast because, every once in a while, before it or we disappeared behind another bend, I could see the trail of dust thrown into the air as it swerved on and off the road. We saw the car several more times before I realized how close it had become, and that at the next bend we were going to meet it face to face.

I knew the car was out of control because the sky above it was heaving with dust. When we came around the last curve I could see the car barrelling end over end toward us, but instead of going out over the edge the car crossed in front of us and hit the side of the mountain. The accident seemed like a physical impossibility, but it happened. As it hit the mountain the impact threw the passenger out through the windscreen and headfirst into a wall of jagged rock. When we stopped, I ran back and found him on the ground, not far from the car. He was still breathing, but his head was caved in on one side. Inside the car, the driver was slumped unconscious against the steering wheel. Our driver wanted to keep going and he would have had I not pleaded: "Peter, for heaven's sake make him to stop. We can't leave them." The driver pulled over to let me out, but he wanted to leave straight away. He insisted that we should continue on to the next town to report the accident; except the next town was at least an hour away. For me it was monstrous to abandon people who were badly injured and defenceless.

The driver of the wrecked car was younger than us, perhaps early thirties. Both the men were short, stocky and rugged, with sun-darkened skin. Their hair was short, black and bristly like a chimney brush. We were afraid to move the man at my feet, so I stayed with him while Peter and our driver climbed higher up the road, hoping that one of their cellular phones would get a signal to call for help. They gestured to me that they were still out of range, and they remained where they were, discussing what to do next. The driver still wanted to leave, but Peter knew I wouldn't go with them.

There was nothing else for me to do except pray for a miracle. It was traumatic to be left alone with the injured man. I paced the ground in front of him and worried: "What will I do if he regains consciousness, perhaps just long enough to whisper his last words, maybe a loving message for his family or friends?" His message would be lost, because I wouldn't understand what he was saying! It might frighten him to death to wake and find a tall blond stranger staring down at him with pale cerulean eyes, and ghostly white skin, speaking in another tongue. So as much as my prayers were

16

for him to regain consciousness, I secretly hoped he might be able to postpone it for a bit.

I related to the man on the ground. I knew that if I were in his position my only chance of survival would be dependent on the kindness of strangers. I believe in karma, so I wasn't about to desert them. As soon as a car came I waved it down. There wasn't anything they could do, but they pulled over to help. None of us wanted to abandon the injured men, so they stayed with me. Then a large truck came along, but the driver didn't stop. He slowed down and looked, but he kept going. Then, as if out of nowhere, more cars appeared and people stopped to see what was going on. There was no longer space to pull over safely.

By this time our driver had had enough. He was afraid that with so many cars blocking the road on a dangerous curve there was going to be another accident. He walked over and started screaming at the driver of the wrecked car, who was just regaining consciousness: "Look at the problems you have caused! You're drunk! Look! You miserable bastard, you have killed your friend." The driver of the wrecked car was pinned, trapped behind the steering wheel, and was just barely conscious when our driver suddenly lost control and slapped him across the face. He shouted: "Look at the suffering you've caused, you "huevon borracho" - "son of a bitch" - damn idiot drunk."

I had never seen a person so close to death and there was no way to call for help. We were so far out of reach we might as well have been on the moon. A man was dying next to us, but there was no sense of panic in the people around me. The situation was out of our hands and they duly accepted it as such. Now that the road was littered with cars, I worried that the driver was right and that perhaps we should have kept going. We hadn't helped, other than collecting a group of people so the men were not alone. When a taxi stopped and the driver told us he would report the accident in the next town we agreed it was time to go. Peter went over to tell the others we were leaving, and that we would report the accident in Tarma, which was in the opposite direction from where the taxi headed. I took my last look at the man, and saw he was still breathing. As I turned to leave an old woman pulled a greasy rag off the floor of a truck and laid it across his head. Maybe his wound was too horrible for her to look at, but it seemed more like the only gesture of kindness she could think of.

It took us an hour to reach Tarma and more time to find the police station. An officer was sitting outside, tipped back in a chair, reading the paper. He glanced up and listened to our story, but when he heard the number of the marker where the crash occurred, he said, "It is out of my jurisdiction." And he turned back to reading his paper. There was nothing we could do, so we went to lunch and afterwards we left for Lima. None of us wanted to stay longer and risk driving through the mountains in the dark. On the trip home, we were shocked to find ourselves blocked behind a truck towing the crashed car. Judging by their driving, they had probably attended the same party as the earlier occupants. The car was tied close behind the dilapidated truck, and sitting in the front seat were two youths struggling to steer it around the curbs. I couldn't imagine there was enough of value in the wrecked car for them to take such an insane risk. The car was shaking to pieces as it wove down the road, and if either vehicle went over the edge it would almost certainly pull the other over with it. We were greatly relieved when we found somewhere to pass and get out of their way. We had seen enough bodies for one day.

Ana, Nicky's nanny in London, was Peruvian, and the next morning Peter rang her family to say we were in Lima and that we had brought a package for them. Her father was happy to hear from us, and he arranged to pick up the package the following day. He also wanted to see Nicky, who they had met with Yesenia on our first trip to Ancon. He asked Peter, "Would it be alright to bring a few tiny gifts for you to take back to Ana." Unlike me, Peter finds it hard to say no, but he was in shock when they arrived carrying two duffle bags stuffed full of things, mostly food, for us to take to her in London. There were several two-litre bottles of Inca Cola, grains, blue corn, ahi, chilli pepper, and other Peruvian foods that weigh a ton, leak, and tend to fall under forbidden agricultural products on the Customs form. Which gave Peter an excuse to say no to almost everything except the clothes. He was excited to see Nicky, and as a special surprise, invited him to come and stay the night with them. He wanted Nicky to meet the rest of their family, and in the morning take him to a local fiesta. Nicky begged us to let him go. Peter hired a cab to take them home and said we would collect Nicky the following day.

When we arrived to pick Nicky up he was excited, and wanted to show us everything in the house. The first thing he showed me were the Christmas photos of him that Ana had sent her family over the years. Peter talked with the family members while Nicky took me around the house to see their pets. He brought me to the kitchen and pointed at a plastic carrier bag hanging against the back of a chair. I had a feeling Nicky was up to something. As we entered the kitchen the bag jumped. It startled me, and I screamed. Everyone rushed in to see what had happened. They laughed when they saw me staring at the bag, which was now moving all over the place. Something was struggling to get free. I thought Nicky was playing a joke and that he had put a kitten in the bag, and before anyone could stop me I reached over to take it out. This time I had an even greater shock and flung myself backwards trying to get away. When I opened the bag I saw what looked like the black beady eyes of an enormous rat, frantically jumping toward me, trying to make its escape. Everyone thought this was enormously funny, except me. When I recovered I asked Nicky, "Oh my God, is it a rat? What is it? Why is it in their kitchen?" Then Peter came in and told me, "No, it isn't a rat. It's a guinea pig and it's probably their supper." At first it seemed as if everyone was going along with the joke, but they weren't. The guinea pig really was for supper, and I got the distinct impression he was somehow already painfully aware of his fate.

Guinea pigs are commonly raised as food in Peru. They are cheap, prolific, and easy to rear at home, providing a good source of lean protein. Large ones can weigh up to four pounds, and they are often sold in markets and restaurants, but mostly in the highland regions of the Andes, where millions of guinea pigs are consumed every year. Usually they are served slit down the middle, disembowelled and deep-fried, their arms and legs spread-eagle across the plate, their astonished rat-like faces peering up as if to say, "Why me?"

That was the first time Nicky had seen a guinea pig. After that he begged us to buy him one for a pet.

BACK IN LIMA

I was thrilled to be back in Lima. It was a relief to wake up late and to be free from my daily routine of early morning school runs and paying bills. Everything in Lima felt new and exciting. Giannina invited me to lunch and introduced me to Marilu, her niece, who lived around the corner from where we were renting and had a daughter Nicky's age. During lunch, I asked if they knew about the fortune-teller, who was supposedly famous in Lima for reading the future. They didn't but they could tell I wanted to have my fortune told, so Marilu phoned some friends to see if she could find out about her for me and get her phone number. Later she spoke to the fortune-teller and made an appointment for me, and that was when she discovered that the woman didn't speak English. So Marilu and Giannina offered to take me and to translate.

The fortune-teller lived in an unfamiliar part of Lima, and we didn't bring a map. We got lost and circled around for ages trying to find her place. Her neighbourhood looked poor, and was devoid of trees. Three blondes arriving in a Mercedes stood out, making me feel conspicuously out of place. We announced ourselves over an intercom which had recently been welded between the bars to keep it from being stolen.

The fortune-teller's maid buzzed us through the security gates into a small open space. We followed the passageway to a communal courtyard that smelled of detergent and boiled potatoes until we came to a door that was open. But as soon as we entered her apartment, the fortune-teller shouted at Giannina: "Get out!" she told her, "You don't belong here, it's in your face." Then she blocked the doorway with her short, stocky frame, insisting that Giannina wait in the courtyard.

I was shocked by her reaction, but Giannina found it amusing and she waited outside while Marilu was allowed in to translate. The flat was small, neat and nondescript. There was nothing to show that this woman was famous or that she had probably amassed a small fortune through her profession. There was nothing particularly notable about her either, except her supreme confidence, which I wouldn't have expected from a woman with her looks and living in her neighbourhood.

After a few minutes Marilu and the fortune-teller argued again. I was afraid I had caused the problem by being there and offered to leave, but Marilu assured me the fortune-teller was upset with Giannina, not me. She didn't want Giannina inside because her negative energy might interfere with my reading. It was true Giannina didn't believe in fortune-tellers, but she hadn't uttered a word before the woman boldly blocked her from entering.

When the fortune-teller calmed down, she told me to hold two cigarettes together and smoke them. We didn't have any cigarettes so she asked me for some change and sent her maid out to buy the two that were needed. I puffed on the cigarettes, and when the ashes reached the crucial length she knocked them off onto a tray and read my future. Then she and Marilu quarrelled again. It was unsettling to have them arguing about something to do with me in a language that I didn't understand. The fortune-teller insisted that Marilu tell me something, but Marilu wouldn't say it. I begged her, "What did she tell you?" After a pause, Marilu gathered courage and, as quickly as she could release the words, said, "The fortune-teller told me your marriage won't last another six months and you will move to Lima." This came as such a surprise, and a relief, that I laughed. The fortune-teller, who was watching, laughed too. I knew my marriage was over. It had been for some time. I just hadn't wanted to admit it and go through another divorce. Marilu had no idea my marriage was in trouble and that I was deeply unhappy. I never discussed my private life. Even with my secret exposed, I was reticent to speak. So Marilu was quite taken aback when I confided that everything the fortune-teller had told her about my marriage, and my situation, was true.

Her predicting a divorce didn't surprise me. Peter and I had little if anything in common. It was as if fate had thrown us together to have a child, and nothing more. But when she insisted I would move to Peru I started to doubt her. It was such an outlandish thing to say. Nevertheless, I was intrigued, and once she said it, it lodged in my brain. The more I thought about it, the more it made sense. Peru seemed like the perfect place to bring up Nicky. She might have said, "You will divorce, and move to another country." After all, I was a foreigner living in London. It's easy for a fortune-teller to guess a woman is having problems with her marriage. Most of the women I know only consult a fortune-teller when they are falling out of love with their husbands, changing their career, or checking out a new lover. Predicting a divorce is a safe guess. But she insisted I would move to Lima, which didn't follow the norm or make sense. Lima has few foreign women moving there without their husbands or a family connection, or because of work, or drawn there by a Peruvian lover. She was adamant what she said was true, and I listened; she had told me so many details about my life that no one else knew. She also said I would be happy in Lima, which was the clincher.

I was at the age that if I didn't do something drastic to change my life I probably never would. If I was going to break the pattern of my life, the time had come. I found it difficult being a wife and a mother, constantly conforming to other people's needs, and I felt guilty that I didn't find my life at all fulfilling. I had everything I had once dreamed of, but there was a void. I found myself trapped and disillusioned by what had once been my greatest desire and I needed to escape, not from my child or my marriage, but from the situation and the monotonous mind-numbing repetition surrounding my life. Sometimes I watched Peter walking down the hallway, dragging his finger along the radiator tops checking for dust. He often talked about his perfectionist American mother with affection, and how, as a child, he had prided himself in keeping his Dinky Toy car collection lined up on shelves in serried ranks alongside his trains. He never talked about playing with his toys, only that they remained in order, untouched. Their strict regimentation was his pleasure. I found his childhood memories oppressive.

His personality hadn't changed much since his youth nor had mine. I had never lined up anything in my life, and I often wondered what it was that had attracted us so passionately to one another. Still, we were friends, and under different circumstances we might have stayed together, though that was not to be our fate. Albert Einstein said: "Insanity: Doing the same thing over and over again and expecting different results." I didn't want to wonder how different my life might have been if only I had had the guts to take a risk and try something new. Nor did I want to live and die with the regret that I hadn't tried for something better. So the idea of divorcing and moving to Peru gained strength.

PETER RETURNS TO LONDON

Peter left Lima and went back to work. Nicky and I had no reason to leave, so we stayed a few weeks longer. That's when I started telling Giannina and Marilu that Nicky and I were moving to Peru. They laughed at me. "The gringa is moving to Lima," they would tell their friends. It was a joke; no one, including myself, really believed it would happen. The idea was so far-fetched and insane that I might fantasize about the move but I wouldn't go ahead with it. Nevertheless, they took me to see several houses for sale. Giannina also managed to get Nicky an appointment at an English school, and booked a car to take us.

The drive to the school took an hour. There was heavy traffic and our driver got lost. It was a bad start. From outside it looked more like a high-security prison than a school. We were required to present identification to a guard before we were allowed to enter. This was a legacy from when terrorism was rife in Peru and, although the protection is no longer entirely necessary, it is good security and remains in place. Nicky was irritable from the drive and he had no desire to see the school or meet with a teacher. He wanted to be with his friends and, after seeing the outside of the building, he wouldn't get out of the car.

I couldn't go in and leave Nicky alone with the driver, who I didn't know, and the guard at the gate didn't speak English, so I couldn't explain my situation and ask him to cancel the appointment for me. Plus we were leaving for London in a few days, and I knew if Nicky didn't come in now it would be impossible to get another appointment. I talked to Nicky and tried to persuade him to come with me. I pleaded with him, but he was on the verge of tears and it didn't seem right to drag him into the school in that state. I sat beside him, disheartened, wondering what to do next.

Our driver sensed there was a problem and he turned around to help. He was rough looking, dark and weather beaten, with deep lines etched across his face; he took up far more than his fair share of the front seat. As he turned toward us I could see he had a kind face. He started talking to Nicky in Spanish, in such a gentle reassuring tone that it was a surprise when he spoke. His voice was soft and rhythmic like a song, incongruous with his hands and face. I found it hard to imagine such a strong, tough looking man possessing such compassion and sensitivity to a child. He said to Nicky, "Why do you cry? Schools are fun; you can make friends and play. Listen, I hear laughter. Go in and see for yourself; they have games and toys. There is nothing out here to play with. And look, I happen to have a packet of sweets in my pocket that I will save for you and give you when you return." After the driver finished talking Nicky jumped out of the car and pulled me toward the school.

The interview didn't go well. In fact, it was a disaster. But the driver made such an impression on me. How he had instinctively tried to help. People in Peru found it natural to get involved, instead of turning away, fearing that they might be intrusive. The world I grew up in was different. I was taught: "Mind your own business, don't interfere - and stay out of anything that doesn't concern you." Those were messages ingrained in me. It was acceptable to show compassion towards something on television or privately.

Distance was the key. It couldn't be misconstrued, or make people feel awkward and uncomfortable; distance was all-important.

Moving to Peru seemed like such a crazy thing to do, but it also made sense and the idea was never far from my thoughts. I loved the lifestyle in Lima; families were close, people were kind and they had excellent schools. I played the idea over and over in my head, convincing myself that, if things didn't work out, we could always go back to London. Nicky was only four years old. He hadn't started kindergarten; if I was going to make a move the timing was right. My idea was to live in Lima until Nicky turned eight and then we would move back so he could finish his schooling in England. The plan seemed so logical it became my solution. Nicky spoke Spanish, which would make it easier for him to fit in. Everything fell into place for the move. But, as my plan progressed, the more terrified I became, and the more desperately I clung to the life I knew. My sense of adventure had long since gone, and in its place was a sense of fear and dread of anything different or unknown.

RETURNED TO LONDON

As soon as Nicky and I got back to London, I told Peter I wanted a divorce. We had talked about it before, so it wasn't a complete surprise. The difference was that this time he knew I meant it. I also told him I wanted to move to Peru, which he hadn't expected. I knew he wouldn't beg me to change my mind and stay, but I had hoped there would be a small show of emotion; perhaps anger, not a total agreement on the subject. His indifference fortified my resolve to leave. Peter and I married each other relatively late in life, in our early forties, the second time round for both of us. We were two diametrically opposite people, but both recently divorced, and lonely. We were the cliché of "opposites attract." However, most of those relationships don't work and when the novelty wore off we drove each crazy.

Peter was born in Chile, surrounded by thousands of acres. When he turned five his Anglophile father had felt it was time to get serious about his education and Peter was sent by ship, accompanied by his nanny, to begin his formal education in an English boarding school. Peter quickly threw his teddy bear away and learned to bury his emotions. He spent all his formative years at boarding school, where he learnt English, and to toughen up. "Suffer in silence" was his motto. And he did. He can separate and detach, often appearing cold and remote. Sentimentality drives him crazy, and I am the epitome of sentimental. He was also a master at changing subjects, so we rarely argued. I often gave vent to angry frustration, trying to break through, but I never did. So nothing was ever resolved between us, which caused an underlying tension from things left unsaid.

Peter worked and lived in Lima years before we met. He knew Nicky would be happy there and that we would have a wonderful life. In the end Peter was supportive of the move. Even though it would be a long and strenuous commute for him to visit Nicky, he agreed to everything. When all of the details were settled, I rang our lawyer and told him Peter and I wanted a divorce. Since neither of us was asking the other for money, he agreed to handle the case; he said the marriage would be dissolved as soon as he could get a court date. The one thing Peter asked of me was that I didn't tell anyone about the divorce; not just yet. Even as Peter and I made plans to separate, we carried on with the marriage and our lives, pretending nothing had changed.

All Nicky talked about was getting a guinea pig. He had his heart set, and we were feeling guilty about the divorce, so we thought it might soften the blow to give him a pet. Nicky chose a guinea pig with long white fur and a large spot surrounding his left eye and called him Spot. But Spot wasn't gentle or tame. He hated to be held or touched, and he escaped several times, hiding under the dishwasher, which had to be professionally removed to get him out safely. Nicky was constantly opening the cage to hold him, and that's when Spot would escape. It was a losing battle to confine him, so I told Peter: "Take the damn thing back, and give it away." I couldn't cope.

I told Nicky that, "Spot had to go back to his family because they missed him so much." Several weeks later we were driving with our friend Saad, who asked about Spot. Nicky told him, "I couldn't keep him." Saad was surprised. Nicky said, "I gave him back because Mummy told me his family missed him so much." Instead of commiserating with Nicky over the loss of Spot our friend told Nicky, "I will buy you a puppy," and he gave me a look that allowed no objection.

I felt anything would be better than bringing a guinea pig to Peru. I had dreaded ringing the airlines or the Peruvian Embassy to find out what papers and vaccinations would be needed to bring Spot into a country where guinea pigs were normally served deep-fried. It would be like flying a chicken to Malaysia as a pet.

A few weeks later, Nicky arrived home with a pug. He insisted on keeping the name Spot, and the name stuck, much to the consternation of the breeder, who felt the name Prince would be considerably better suited to one of her champion pugs.

Spot arrived in the middle of all the chaos: our getting a divorce; packing; sorting through years of collected books, papers and clothes that needed to be thrown out or given away; simultaneously keeping the rooms tidy for prospective buyers of the flat, who came traipsing through with their estate agents at all hours of the day. I was mentally and physically exhausted, and a new puppy, which greedily chewed everything within reach and flooded the kitchen floor with its inexhaustible reserves of pee, was a not altogether welcome burden to cope with.

THE FLAT SOLD SO QUICKLY

I t was difficult to pretend that we were still a family while the movers were packing up our home. There were pink and blue labels stuck to everything, identifying who owned what. Strangers were taking paintings off the wall and putting them into crates. Peter was at his office, and I mechanically went from room to room trying to make sure the boxes were labelled correctly so that they would arrive at the right places. I was numb, watching Peter's and my past being ripped apart and then neatly separated and packed away. I wanted to beg them to stop, but the flat had already sold. It wasn't until our Porter came in to say goodbye that I could no longer contain my grief.

I had first lived in the building years before I met Peter, when I lived there with my mother. Our Porter, Mr. Whitaker, was my dear friend. He used to sing 'Bye Bye Blackbird' to me and smuggled my boyfriends out the back door when I was young. This time when I saw him was when everything fell apart. He asked me, "How's it going then?" and I found I couldn't speak. I wanted to tell him, "Not so well Mr. Whitaker," but in that split second of kindness I let down my guard, and all the devastation and sadness come pouring out of me so fast that I couldn't contain it. There was no chance to recover my composure before I buried my face against his chest and fell to pieces. Mr. Whitaker put his arm around me and gently led me to the other room, away from the men packing, and held me until I could pull myself together. Afterwards I told him, "That was a relief." We laughed. "So much for your stiff upper lip," he said, and I went back in, to finish what I was doing.

No one had predicted that the flat would sell so quickly. It sold in weeks, not months as we initially expected. Originally I planned to rent somewhere after it sold and stay in London for several months or longer, to give us time to adjust, but I was so overwhelmed by the divorce and the move I hadn't even looked for a rental. Peter had moved into another flat, but Nicky, Ana, and I had nowhere to go.

It had never occurred to me it would be difficult to rent a flat, but it was. Toddlers and puppies are notoriously unpopular with owners and rental agents. Every place that allowed children and pets was badly furnished and depressing, especially compared to our flat, which I had loved. I became more and more desperate for the three of us. We were in a state of limbo; I wasn't sure when Nicky and I were leaving for Lima, or if we would stay in London and rent. I didn't have a plan. Fortunately, the man who bought our flat let us stay for a couple more weeks, which was our saving grace. I needed more time to come to terms with everything before leaving for Peru. I had lived most of my adult life in London, and I wanted time to say goodbye to my friends.

There was no furniture left in the flat except for a few odds and ends, and the beds. Everything was packed and ready for shipping to Peru. It was a bit of a relief to be unburdened from all our possessions. Nicky could run around and enjoy the simpler life, but being there was a constant reminder that this was no longer our home, where we were now guests, with nowhere to go. Knowing that there was no turning back was never far from my thoughts; nor was my guilt, wondering, "What have I done?"

My friends were supportive and seemed to admire me for my daring sense of adventure. No one in our group had divorced, uprooted and started over in a country they didn't know. Who in their right mind would choose to step into the great unknown, leaving their safe comfortable life to raise a child on their own, especially at my age? It made me appear daring and unconventional, which in fact I wasn't; it was all bravado and bluff. In truth, I was hoping for a saviour and a way back to the security we were about to leave. During conversations, I steered clear of painful subjects. I numbed myself with wine while trying to fool myself I was excited about the move, even though I knew I wasn't. My last days in London were filled with lunches and dinners, saying goodbye to old friends, and distracting myself from the move. Never allowing myself time to think.

I became desperate as our grace period in the flat was coming to an end. I hadn't found anywhere to rent in London; I hadn't really looked. I wandered around aimlessly, incapable of organizing or accomplishing anything. Then a few days before we had to leave the flat, Giannina rang to say she had found us a place to rent in Lima. She told me, "It is perfect for you. If you are interested you must tell me straight away, or someone else will take it." There were no other options available so I said, "Yes," and rang the airlines to book our tickets to Peru.

There had been many goodbyes in the past few weeks, but nothing prepared me for the goodbye at the airport. Nicky was crying and clinging to his father, and for a moment I didn't think he would leave his father and go with me. He was also leaving Ana, who had been with him since he was a few months old. I was no longer sure it was right to be taking Nicky so far away from his father, or that moving to Peru was the solution. I put on a big show, pretending to be excited about the move, but in reality, I was petrified. At times, the stress made me struggle to breathe. I envied everyone in their secure homes and marriages, even the ones that I knew weren't happy. At least they were together and maintained some semblance of a normal existence. I hated myself for being the cause of this disruption and wondered what was so special about my unhappiness that we needed to move Peru.

I also felt responsible. I needed to show Nicky an example of dealing with problems in a positive way, instead of retreating to bed and hiding from the world, which is what I longed to do. I wanted to disappear until this problem somehow resolved itself or blew over, as I did when I was young. Nicky wasn't fooled by the masquerade; he could feel something wasn't right. We were living apart from his father, and only the two of us were moving to Peru. The situation didn't make sense, but neither of us talked to Nicky about the separation. Peter and I continued pretending to be a family even when we were saying goodbye at the airport.

Peter kissed us goodbye. He told Nicky, "I love you. I will see you and Mummy in Miami very soon, and we will all go to Lima together."

Up until that moment travel and airports had been a source of fun and adventure, something we looked forward to. Ana insisted on taking a photo before Nicky and I went through passport control. Peter stood beside Nicky; we posed, smiling, with Nicky between us. But it wasn't a happy photo. Nicky looked bewildered, revealing a despair that should never be seen on a child's face.

Yet there was also this faint little voice inside my head, cheering me on as we made our way toward the gate, telling me, "Yes! Here are your spirit and your strength back." My other voice, the much louder and less positive one, was saying something quite different. It was a constant battle to maintain my equilibrium while trying to figure out which voice was really my own.

Florida

Our first stop was Florida. I wanted to break the trip up and say our goodbyes to my mother. On reflection, I was stalling for time and hoping that someone would try and talk me out of what was beginning to feel like the most foolhardy, insane idea I had ever

34

had in my life. Secretly, since no one else had tried to stop me, I was counting on my mother to do so.

When we arrived at Tampa airport, Nicky and I searched for her. She had promised to meet us, and I was devastated not to find her there, waiting when we got off the plane. Our porter piled the luggage into a small mountain near one of the exit doors and then left. We were so overburdened with baggage it was impossible to move without help. In addition Spot hadn't been out of his cage since London, and he was beginning to be very vocal about needing to do something in the bathroom department, but there was no way of taking him outside without leaving Nicky alone with the luggage. I had forgotten to bring a bag to pick up his poop. Spot was going to have to suffer along with the rest of us. I just wished he would do so in silence.

There was an unspoken fear between us. Where was Grandma? Why wasn't she at the airport waiting to pick us up? Had she crashed? Was she hurt? Had she forgotten us? How could she do this to us? I felt an overwhelming desire to cry, but I knew it would only make things worse by upsetting Nicky. When Nicky was upset, he usually responded by behaving horribly, which was the last thing I needed. Children hate to see their parents in this frazzled state. With good reason I suppose; because if we fall apart and can't take care of ourselves then who is going to protect and take care of them?

People could see we were having problems, but they kept their distance. My desperation frightened them away. We looked lost, sitting there with a mountain of luggage and Spot crying to get out of his cage. I tried to be positive by reminding myself this was an exciting adventure, even though it wasn't true. Then I remembered an article I had read that said it was good for you to smile, and that by smiling you used fewer facial muscles than when frowning. It also went on to say, "you could trick your brain by smiling," because it would connect the signals from the muscular configuration, i.e. I smile, therefore I must be happy. My smile probably looked grotesque, and it wasn't fooling anyone, least of all Nicky or me. He might have thought I had become deranged when he saw me smiling. Sometimes there comes a point where there really isn't much to smile about; unless you've lost your mind. Then my positive voice would kick in saying, "Oh! For heaven sake, all you have to do is go over and ring your mother and rent a car. What is the big deal?" But when I turned back and saw the luggage, the weight of my problems pulled me back to earth and I started smiling again.

It was impossible for me to carry everything over to the phone, and Nicky was too young to leave alone with the luggage. I was afraid to leave Spot and the luggage alone; it might look suspicious and create a panic, or be stolen. We had just left London where security is tight. England has lived with terrorism for years, so the public is vigilant and reports any parcels or luggage left unattended. Bomb squads are trained and ready to explode anything that looks abandoned or suspicious, especially in airports and public places.

We couldn't remain in the airport forever. I told Nicky, "I need your help. I have to ring Grandma. Please stay with the luggage. If someone talks to you and tries to get you to leave or tries to get you to come with them for any reason, shout and I'll come running." After that I ran to the phone and rang my mother. There was no response, so I left a message saying, "Mummy we are at the airport. I must have given you the wrong day." Then I ran back to Nicky.

I was exhausted and stressed out from the separation, the move, the flight, no sleep, and not finding my mother. I felt as if one more problem would push me over the edge. The strain of the past few weeks had shattered me. I collapsed on the bench next to Nicky and smiled as memories of my father flooded my consciousness.

Nicky was bored, and while I was planning our next move he started fiddling with the door of Spot's cage. The police had warned us in Customs not to let Spot loose in the airport. The last time Nicky opened the cage door, he escaped. I worried Nicky would let him loose again, but I couldn't help but think it might be to my advantage. If the police came to arrest me, at least there would be someone to help with the luggage!

My father had often teased my mother saying, "I would never worry about someone kidnapping our children, but if they did, they would pay us to take them back. Of course, they would have to find me first!" After all of these years, I laughed at his joke. I had become the parent of a child just like me, and suddenly I understood exactly how he felt. All I had to do was to figure out how to get our luggage to the car rental counter, and from there to the rental car, without help. There wasn't a porter in sight. As I did my last disheartened search to find one, I saw my mother. I burst out, "Oh my God, there's Mummy! Nicky look, it's Granny!" People turned in our direction and looked at us. Nicky and I were thrilled when she rushed over and hugged us, telling us she had been waiting at the gate but somehow, she hadn't seen us when we left the airplane. I have never been so happy, or relieved, to see anyone in my life.

The next problem was fitting the luggage in her car, and it took several attempts to arrange everything. Spot's cage didn't fit, so we dismantled it; plus we had hand luggage, a collapsible bicycle and all our cases. At one point it looked as if I would have to rent a car for the luggage and follow them to Sarasota, but eventually, after putting suitcases where my feet should have been, and my feet up somewhere up around my ears, we got everything in and we were on our way. Other than a great feeling of relief, I couldn't help but think that this was only the beginning of our journey—the easy part.

We weren't even in Peru yet.

MY MOTHER

My mother is a staunch New Yorker, thirteenth generation, Dutch descended and proud of it. Her family wintered in Florida, where they kept a home. It was where she met my father, who had escaped New York after a messy divorce. I was born in Florida. I ought to have been a fourteenth generation New Yorker, had I not been born in January, the coldest month. My brothers shared my fate, all of us being born on the same day, in the same month, but in different years.

Much to the horror of my grandmother, Mother didn't go back to New York to give birth, so along with my brothers I became the first and only generation to be born in Florida; thus breaking hundreds of years of family tradition. Grandma once commiserated with me: "Your mother has a stubborn streak. Imagine giving birth in Sarasota, a circus town with pretty beaches. You are the only native-born Floridians I know." Which caused me to feel both rootless and spiritually misplaced.

My father was older than my mother by fifteen years. She was his second wife, technically his third if you count that he married

his first wife twice. With whom he had two kids. We grew up together in the same house and we were very close, except in age,
which added to my youthful confusion. Same father but different
mothers, in an era where divorce was taboo, and children were
discouraged from asking questions.

My mother listened to all my fears about moving to Peru, but
contrary to what I had expected she was excited about the move.
She felt that it would be a wonderful experience, and if things
didn't work out we were free to move back to London. Nicky's
school had agreed to save his place for two years, so we hadn't
burnt any bridges. We could always go home. She reminded me we
had moved to London when she was my age, in her late forties, and
that the experience had enriched our lives. London was a more
conservative choice than Peru, and we spoke the same language,
but even so that move, with all its changes and challenges, wasn't
easy. My parents moved to London not knowing a single person,
and with three disgruntled teenagers in tow, who had left their
lifelong friends behind, and had nothing in common between
them. But it was an exciting time to be alive, and to be in London.

A few months after the move to London, my maternal grandmother died unexpectedly, and my parent's marriage of almost
twenty-five years started to break up. As a family, we weren't much
support to each other. Instead, being out of our familiar surroundings and routine, I became conscious of how very different we were
from each other. I didn't have friends in London, and because I
had nothing in common with my brothers I couldn't take refuge
in their company, which forced me to become independent. Each
of us reacted differently to our new environment; we formed independent friendships, pursued our separate interests, and eventually each of us headed in a separate direction.

The weather in Sarasota was ideal. Nicky and I swam and took
long walks with Spot. It was a world away from the dark winter
weather and the chaos of London that we had left behind. So much

so that I considered staying. Nicky was smiling again, a far cry from how he looked on the flight over. But Sarasota was no longer my home, nor was it the same town I remembered with its miles of deserted beaches. The vast open spaces had all but disappeared. Most of the landmarks I grew up with were replaced, and I was out of touch with most of my childhood friends. I knew that if I stayed it wouldn't be like returning home, it would be starting over in a town where little was familiar and all that remained were memories. Reminding me that there is no going back. Life changes. Plus I had started renting the flat in Lima. I began to finalise our plans to leave, Nicky wasn't yet enrolled in a school.

Most schools in Lima begin in March, contra season. Nicky was starting Kindergarten, so the timing wasn't crucial; nevertheless, we felt it would be harder for him to arrive after the other children had settled in and made friends. My mother wished us luck as we left for the airport and sent us off with her blessing.

Ready or not, here we come!

ARRIVE IN PERU

When Nicky saw Peter at Miami airport he broke loose from my hand and shot across the room, colliding with his father at full speed and, for the longest time, he remained wrapped around his legs, not daring to let go.

I was grateful Peter was coming with us. It wasn't easy for him to leave London, it was a long trip and he had a company to run. At that time travelling with computers, and the Internet wasn't yet commonplace, which made it difficult for him to work from Lima.

We arrived in Lima late at night and were met at the airport by a driver and Yesenia, Ana's sister, who we had hired temporarily to look after Nicky. They chatted away in Spanish. Neither the driver nor Yesenia spoke English, so I was unable to communicate with them. Giannina had the keys to our flat, and we stopped at her house to pick them up. It was almost midnight by then, and she was leaving early in the morning for the States. It was too late to talk. We kissed hello, she handed me the keys and promised to ring the minute she returned to Lima, and then she hurried back to bed.

The Porter was waiting inside, drowsing off in the entrance; he woke and opened the door when he heard us climbing the steps. Peter, Nicky and I crowded into the lift, and he followed us up with Yesenia and the luggage. The flat hadn't been opened for some time, and as we entered we were hit by a wave of stale and uninviting air. I knew nothing about the place, other than it was small, dogs were allowed, and we didn't need a lease.

After our flat in London, this was a rude awakening. Just inside the front door was a narrow passageway leading to the drawing room. On the left there was a kitchen with the laundry room and a maid's bedroom. Our bedrooms were at the far end of the flat, opposite each other. The rooms were nicely proportioned with parquet floors, and the bathrooms had just been renovated, but the whole place would have fit into one room of our London flat, making it feel claustrophobic. The Porter brought the bags to my room, and then he left for bed.

That was when reality struck. I looked over at the un-upholstered foam block which was now my mattress, the wobbly plaster lamp, the scruffy furniture, the grey dusty curtains, and my heart sank. Peter put the nanny in charge of finding the sheets and making beds, while I rushed out to walk Spot. I needed a few minutes alone in order to pull myself together. It was hard to pretend I was happy with our new home. I was exhausted, and the enormity of the move was beginning to sink in. Here I was, walking Spot on an unfamiliar street, in a country where I only had two friends, one of whom was leaving in a few hours for the States. I missed London and everything familiar, but Spot was pleased to be out and he dragged me down the sidewalk, relieving himself and smelling every lamppost along the way. He was happy, the more territory for him to mark the better. I had always taken Spot out when we returned home from parties in London, usually long after midnight. It was peaceful at that hour, when the streets were deserted and the air was fresh.

As we passed the heavily armed guards standing outside one of the Embassies, I noticed they stared in our direction; they seemed curious and surprised to see me walking alone at that hour. And a bit later they must have thought I had lost my mind when I pulled out a plastic bag, stooped down, and then using it like a glove scooped up Spot's poop and took it with me. How was I to know that no sane person in Lima would have picked it up? But at that moment I was still blissfully unaware of how different Lima really was, which was a blessing, because if I had realized all the differences and difficulties I would be faced with, I might have never made the move.

When I returned home, everyone went straight to bed. Nicky was fast asleep as soon as his head touched the pillow. Peter had jetlag and was soon snoring away in the bed next to Nicky, but it was impossible for me to fall asleep. Everything around me was unfamiliar. I looked at the strange new surroundings and at the shadows thrown up on my ceiling from the headlights below; and I listened unwillingly as my mind replayed over and over again, in great detail, every mistake I had ever made in my entire life.

In the morning, I felt mentally and physically drained, and struggled to get out of bed. Nicky was awake. He was in the drawing room with his hands and face glued to the window. I went over to see where he was looking. It was the first time I saw our view in daylight and I was shocked as I looked down on a busy intersection, and the rubbish filled roof of a petrol station.

Directly opposite us was a building with dark filthy windows. It looked derelict. On its roof were two electric billboards that changed pictures every few minutes, advertising something to do with plumbing. In London we overlooked a garden and ornate bridges crossing the River Thames. I was just about to beg Nicky's forgiveness for the move, for the apartment, for everything, when he turned to me with such a happy face and said, "Mummy look, the sign changes, and there is a Burger King across the street. Isn't that great?" He had been at the window all morning. He loved the view. The street was alive with traffic and people. There had been a rear end collision at the traffic light, accompanied by the foulest of language and a fight, Hollywood style. Just outside our window! All very exciting.

Nicky pointed to the vendors for D'Onofrio ice cream, pushing their carts down the sidewalk and tooting their familiar horns. He showed me a woman resting on a low wall near our steps; her heavy basket beside her as she sang, "Come and buy my fresh tamales." Nicky was thrilled with his bedroom, which was huge compared to his bedroom in London; and it had a television. Although it wasn't connected, it was there; and he was sharing a room with his father, which pleased him to no end. Seeing the apartment through his eyes changed my perspective of the place. Everyone had settled in. Peter was at the dining room table, reading the newspaper. By the time I got up, Peter had found the switch for the hot water and had sent Yesenia to the grocery store to buy essentials. She also bought a bag of ripe mangos and freshly baked bread. After I finished breakfast, we started making plans for our first day in Lima.

Our landlady's maid arrived unexpectedly in the afternoon, and asked if she could work for us. She had been out of work since the owner had moved to the US. Peter liked her and suggested I hire her three days a week. She knew the flat and the Porter, and everything around us; she could be a big help. The following week, Gloria, who had looked after Nicky on our last trip and spoke reasonable English, moved in and took over as his nanny.

Now that we had a maid and a nanny in a tiny rented flat, there wasn't anything for me to do other than learn Spanish and buy things for the flat. Our furniture and household things weren't arriving from England for several months. The first thing I bought was a fax machine, and a video player for Nicky. I bought sheets, towels, bedspreads, cutlery, plates, cups, glasses, silver picture frames, and vases. I wanted the flat to feel more like home. We were on the commercial end of a good residential street, and just next to a grocery store, which was very convenient. It was difficult for me to get around Lima on my own. So having most of the essentials within walking distance gave me a small feeling of independence.

I grew to love the flat. It was tiny, unadorned, and comfortable. I no longer worried about Nicky running around, or something getting broken. Nothing was there we couldn't easily replace. In London, our furniture was inherited from Peter's family, or special pieces we collected over the years. Peter was constantly checking the heirlooms for scratches and chips, which became the bane of my existence. The drawing rooms were off limits to Nicky; Peter had them barricaded with childproof gates, so I only used them for entertaining. Most of the time, Nicky and I stayed in the kitchen, where he had an area to play, or in our bedrooms. The rental flat in Lima was a haven. Nicky's toys were scattered around, and he could play where he pleased.

We took it for granted that Nicky would go to the English school where he was interviewed. They had complained that he was very active, but he had tested high and there was no reason to believe he wouldn't be accepted. Peter had corresponded with them from London and in one letter they told us, "We will be happy to take Nicholas, if his school in London can knock off the rough edges." Which seemed an odd comment.

I made another appointment for another interview as soon as we arrived in Lima, but it was a disaster. The woman who met with Nicky told me straight away he wasn't suitable for the school, which was a huge relief because I had reached the same conclusion the moment we spoke. It would have been awkward if I were the one to say no. Albert Einstein said: "It is a miracle that curiosity survives formal education." I knew Nicky wouldn't have thrived there. On the other hand it was daunting, for I hadn't looked at the other schools and Peter had a limited time left in Lima. I had no idea what to do.

That weekend we were invited to stay with friends at the beach. We must have looked miserable, because the conversation quickly turned to our problem of Nicky's school. Marilu, our hostess, told us her that her son was in an English school, which she recommended. When we showed interest, she set up an appointment for us to meet with the teachers and to see the school, which was light, modern, with playing fields and a swimming pool. And instead of sitting Nicky down for a formal examination, the teacher played games and talked with him to determine his level of knowledge. Nicky liked the school, and was accepted straight away. We were impressed by the woman who interviewed us, and by the setup of the classrooms. The kindergarten was small scale, separate from the upper school, with cosy classrooms overlooking a lake.

All of the classes were taught in English, so Nicky would begin school with a huge advantage.

NICKY IN KINDER IN LIMA

Nicky kissed us goodbye at the door and walked into the classroom. I waited outside thinking he might run back to me, but he didn't. Peter signalled me it was time to leave I followed him to the car, hiding my eyes behind Kleenex and sunglasses. Nicky appeared more confident than most of the other children, who clung to their mothers at the door. By four years old Nicky was a veteran of tumble tots, music classes, and art programs and pre-kinder in London; but for many children there this was the first time they had been separated from their families or nannies, and the first time they had to cope on their own.

Once Nicky had settled into his new school, Peter left for London. Nicky turned five the following week. We planned a party for the following month, when Peter returned to Lima, but in the meantime, we got permission to send Nicky to school with an enormous birthday cake, the largest and most colourful one in the shop. It was decorated with cartoon figures and with an electric car stuck deep into lurid green and blue icing. This allowed

Nicky to celebrate with other children, but his real birthday was on Saturday, so I bought another cake and invited Giannina and Marilu over with their daughters.

I included Salvador, a man I had just met through Giannina.

BACK TO THE FORTUNE-TELLER

M y fortune-teller smiled as I entered her room and said, "I'm not surprised to hear you are living in Lima." Later she told me: "I see you are going out with a man." Which was true. I was dating Salvador. The fortune-teller wasn't enthusiastic about him and advised me to get rid of him straight away. There was no hesitation in her counsel. She simply told me he wasn't right for me, end of conversation.

I had met Salvador at Club Waikiki, a surfing club started in the twenties; no riffraff allowed, gentlemen only. Salvador was hosting a lunch for an ambassador who was on my list of introductions. So Giannina brought me along to meet him, and to make some new friends.

Salvador swam over to the table when he saw us, and climbed out of the pool. His toned muscular body glistening wet, I had been watching him swim laps; the Adonis that he was. I knew he was a scoundrel with women even before we met. The fact that he had a terrible reputation with women made him all the more intriguing. Giannina cautioned me that most of his relationships only lasted a few months, but I had no serious intentions, so when the fortune-teller saw my disappointment she looked deep into my future again and said, "Well, okay go ahead enjoy him, just don't get involved. At some point, he will become one of your close friends." All of which turned out to be true.

I was newly divorced, so most of my questions were about love: "Am I going to fall in love?" "Will I stay in Lima forever?" "Will I fall in love with a Peruvian?" She had no answers, except she didn't think he'd be Peruvian and she doubted I would stay there forever. She told me, "Come back and see me in a few months, when things have settled down and there is less disruption in your life." As we were leaving she stopped me. She hesitated, and then, as if it were no more than a thought out loud, she said: "You won't be a multi-millionaire. But everything will be alright."

It seemed like an odd thing for her to say, as it had nothing to do with our conversation. I hadn't asked her about money. I thought, "Well she certainly got that wrong. The one concern I didn't have was money." A second later she surprised me again by bringing up another man who had recently taken me to dinner. She smiled and was just about to speak when she changed her mind saying, "Never mind. It's a long and complicated explanation. He is someone important in your life, but now isn't the time to explain. I will tell you about him the next time we meet."

Marilu was translating, and though I was desperate to know what she was going to say, I didn't want to appear too curious by pressing her for more details, especially after she told Marilu, "Tell your gringa that her dinner date is a fabulous lover." I had no idea what she was going to say next, and I thought it best to end the conversation. We kissed goodbye, but I hesitated to leave. There were so many questions burning inside me, but none that I could ask her confidentially.

It was exasperating to leave without knowing what was just on the tip of her tongue.

GLORIA LEAVES TO VOTE

The next major event in Peru was the 2000 presidential elections, the first round on 9th April, the second round on 28th May. Banners were hoisted up and stretched between lamp posts. Trucks drove up and down our street, blasting propaganda from the rival candidates, each one competing to be heard above the others.

Voting is mandatory in Peru. Nicky's nanny was from outside Lima, which was where she was registered to vote. Her bus ride home would take twelve hours, so she had to leave the day before the elections to get there in time. Gloria also asked me if she could spend an extra day with her mother, who she hadn't seen in several years. I agreed, so it would be three or four days before she returned. We had only been living in Lima for a few months, and I was lost without her there to translate. Armandina, who also worked for us, didn't speak English. We said hello when she arrived, but otherwise, we hardly spoke.

Armandina came to work on a Sunday that was an election day. She tried to explain something to me, and I assumed she was telling me she had to leave to vote, which I knew, but Nicky came in to translate and asked if it would be alright if he went with her. I thought they would be back in a couple of hours and that it would be interesting for him so I said yes. Armandina had worked for a friend of Giannina for years, cleaning and looking after her son, so I knew she was reliable.

After waiting hours for them to return, Armandina rang me and put Nicky on the phone. By then it was very late and I had been frantic. When Nicky asked me if he could spend the night at her house, I said, "No, come home immediately." But Nicky wanted to stay, and he told her, "My mummy says yes."

Armandina had no way to know I had said otherwise. She thought I said goodbye to Nicky and hung up the phone. Nicky was having the time of his life playing with children his age at the election party, and he didn't want to leave. I sat clutching the receiver, still not believing they had hung up. Nicky was just five years old, and there was no way for me to reach him. They had called me from a payphone, she didn't own a phone, and I didn't have her address.

I had no idea what to do or where they were. I rang Giannina to ask for help, but her maid who spoke no English answered the phone, and because Giannina wasn't there to take the call, it was impossible for me to leave a message.

I switched on the television to check the election results and found out that Alejandro Toledo, one of the presidential candidates, was now in the lead. That was great news, because Salvador was running for the Senate under Toledo, and he would be pleased. We rarely saw each other these days; Salvador was out campaigning, and I felt lost in large groups because of the language so I stayed home. Toledo wasn't a typical candidate running for president. He grew up in poverty and was the first in his family to attend high school. As a child he helped his family with money earned by selling newspapers and lottery tickets and by shining shoes. After he finished grade school Toledo was expected to work full time, but his father allowed him to continue his education with the proviso that he worked after school to help with expenses. In the mid-sixties, when he won a partial scholarship to study at the University of San Francisco in a program for non-English speakers, money was still tight, and he worked part-time pumping gas while learning English and completing an undergraduate degree. Afterwards he went to Stanford University, where he earned two Masters and a Doctorate.

Toledo was the first indigenous candidate to run for President of Peru, and his same stature and strong Andean features inspired confidence with much of the population. He grew up in poverty like them and knew their problems first hand. They saw a better future with him in power. If he won the election he would give the underprivileged a voice, and a chance to be represented. Toledo cared about his people; he embodied the dream that, regardless of heritage or race, with a good education, hard work and determination you could succeed. He promised to create more jobs, and they believed him. He also stressed his support for decentralisation.

By the time I looked again, Fujimori had shot into the lead. Now tens of thousands of protesters gathered downtown and clashed with riot police. It was a mob scene, with tear gas hanging in the air and projectiles being hurtled in every direction. The centre of Lima looked like a war zone. I sat alone, watching the riots; terrified, not knowing where Nicky was, or if he was safe.

I didn't dare ring Peter for advice because I would have to admit I had lost Nicky. I knew he was at an election party with Armandina, but I didn't know where that was, or how to reach him. I just prayed they weren't near where all the political riots had sprung up. In any case, there was nothing Peter could do, so there was no point in worrying him.

Spot needed to go out, but I stayed near the phone, hoping Nicky might have a change of heart and ring me. I also feared that the rioters might come around the corner at any moment and sweep us away. The television was on, but the only news on the elections was in Spanish. Later, I found an English channel showing more of the riots, but I was not so familiar with Lima to know where they were in relation to where I was or where Nicky might be. I didn't realize that the riots were confined to a small area in the centre of Lima, miles away.

I still really knew nothing about Peruvian politics, other than that there had been much controversy over this election. President Fujimori was running for a third term in office, which was apparently unconstitutional; and three of the constitutional judges who opposed his running for a third term were dismissed. Fujimori had power, and he was going to use whatever it took to get re-elected. Most of the people I talked to admitted he was a tyrant, and they wouldn't want to cross him, but many still supported him. He had ended terrorism and revived the economy; they felt that if a few people had suffered because of his regime, then so be it. It was a small price to pay for the majority who had benefitted. He had done what other governments had been unable to do. Dramatic measures were required to defeat terrorism and regain national stability. There is no clean way to fight terrorism.

The news channels showed large angry mobs rioting in the streets. I switched off the lights and hid behind a curtain to look out, but everything seemed quiet outside. I became restless and thought, since I lived next to a grocery store, why not take advantage of it being there and buy a bottle of wine as a consolation. I crept down the backstairs and peeked through the front door to make sure it was still safe before sprinting the short distance to the entrance of the store. It was an immense relief to be there, surrounded by people shopping and going about their everyday lives. No one appeared anxious or on edge, so I relaxed and took my time to select a good wine. Just as I had taken a bottle from the shelf, a sales assistant started talking to me. I didn't want to appear rude, but I couldn't understand her and I didn't feel like talking. It was also annoying because I assumed she wanted to sell me another brand she was promoting. Companies regularly put salespeople in grocery stores to promote their products, and when they are there, it is impossible to escape them. Customers often took the product and later dumped it in another aisle, because it was easier to take it than to say no.

I told her in English, "This is the wine I want," and I headed toward the cashier. She followed me and became even more persistent. So I told her again, "This is the wine I want," and I pulled it toward my chest. But before it was firmly against me, she surprised me by taking hold of the bottle. Several people gathered around to see what was happening. More were on their way as I continued to resist: "No! This is the wine I want!" I thought, "Bloody hell, this sales girl is too much!"

I knew I couldn't complain as none of the employees there spoke English, so I stood my ground and continued wrestling with her over the bottle. Eventually, a woman in the crowd who spoke a little English stepped forward and gently explained that during the elections no alcohol is sold. I argued that I was foreign and couldn't vote. She graciously held out her hand for the bottle. It was a showdown. She waited; I resisted, until her patience paid off and I handed it over. The small crowd gathered around us nodded sympathetically, they seemed full of suggestions but I couldn't understand them. I went home feeling like a complete idiot; dispirited, childless, and sober, wondering what ever had possessed me to leave England.

Nicky and Armandina returned home early the next morning. I was bleary-eyed, exhausted by broken sleep, and jumped a mile when they entered my room. Nicky was tugging on Armandina's hand, trying to drag her into the kitchen to prepare his breakfast. I was so relieved that they were home that I didn't make a fuss. I hardly said a word, other than to tell Nicky how worried I had been, and to make him promise to never to do something like that again. He shouldn't have stayed with Armandina, but in fact they were never in danger. If I had been able to talk to her myself Armandina would have brought him home.

Now that Nicky was back, life felt, more or less, normal again. He had had fun, being with other children, playing games and watching horror films that were forbidden at home. Nicky described the party and all the friends, family and children who were there. If he had been with me, we would have watched the elections. Ever since Peter left, we hadn't been going out, unless a friend picked us up. I found it difficult getting around Lima on my own. It was easier staying home instead of venturing out and struggling to make myself understood.

DECIDED TO BUY A FLAT

I thought it would be better to buy a place and put down roots rather than to rent. By buying, I demonstrated that we had made a firm commitment to stay. Every day after my Spanish lessons I went to see properties, mostly in San Isidro, which was the obvious choice because my friends lived there and it was the area I knew best. I could walk to almost everything, and there were parks nearby where Nicky could play. I also looked at neighbourhoods closer to Nicky's school, where many of his friends lived, but he was with them all day and I would have been isolated there and I would have needed a car and a driver to get around, which was the last thing I wanted to deal with. In San Isidro, it was easy to catch a cab, and eventually we settled on an apartment.

We didn't choose a house because Lima was unlike other cities, which have rigid building restrictions. In Lima, things changed all the time, including the rules. I have seen beautiful houses disappear without warning, truckloads of men arrive with sledgehammers, and in a few hours the house is gone without a trace. The problem is, once something has been demolished, what the

57

authorities will allow them to build in its place. My dream was to have a house with a garden, but I was persuaded an apartment would be safer. Security is more complicated for a house. I would need guachimán - watchmen - to sit outside the house, night and day, which can also be a problem if you hire the wrong people. Maids can be another problem. They are often naïve and have been known to be seduced by crooks to gain entry into houses while the owners were away. It is safer to live in an apartment with porters who keep an eye on who is coming and going. I wanted a place we could lock up and leave when we travelled, and not worry about it while we were away.

In the end Giannina found us a flat overlooking the Lima Golf Club, a remnant of the English community in Peru. The apartment had full time porters, good security and an exceptional view; the main rooms looked across the trees and ponds of the golf course, and on a clear day you could see the islands off the coast. I was told, "Now is the time to buy property in Lima, prices are at an all-time low," but only one of my offers was accepted. Which was a good sign, expensive properties, were holding their value; even so I had only heard bad news about the economy. It didn't feel like a good time to invest. If I bought an apartment and things didn't work out, we would be trapped in Lima until the economy recovered. And at that time, no one was optimistic about a quick recovery.

BOUGHT A FLAT - MAY 2000

The realtor rang to tell me my offer had been accepted and that I needed to come to the notary's office to sign papers. She told me to bring the deposit in the form of a banker's draft made out in the owner's name.

The prospect of buying a property in Peru was exciting but terrifying. I rang my lawyer and let him know my offer had been accepted, and that we needed to meet at the notary with the deposit. I told him, "The day they've chosen isn't good for me, it's Mother's Day. I have a breakfast date at Nicky's school, and I can't be late."

He said, "Don't worry. I will arrange for the meeting to be early so you will have plenty of time to sign the papers and get to the school."

I arrived at the notary's office early and found the receptionist didn't speak English, so there was no way of explaining to her why I was there. She didn't appear to recognize any of the names on my papers, but she didn't mind me standing there, so I waited next to her desk hoping for a familiar face, or someone who would recognize me when they came in. It was nerve-racking to be there alone, but it was too early to have asked a friend to come with me.

I had never bought a flat on my own before, and I expected my lawyer to be there to guide me through the legal procedures. I was jittery from lack of sleep and had been tossing and turning all night. My mind stayed wide-awake, thinking and rethinking, weighing up all the pros and cons of buying a flat in Peru. It was exciting, but also worrying to take on such an enormous financial commitment in a country which I hardly knew.

I was under pressure to get to Nicky's school. It would be unforgivable to be late, and for him to be the only child in his kindergarten class without their mother. In the far corner of the room I saw an attractive couple, a father and his daughter, talking and sorting through papers. After observing me for a few minutes they came over and introduced themselves in English and asked if I was the one buying her flat. I said, "Yes, I think so." I showed them my file and asked, "Can we sign the papers and get this over with. I want to leave for my son's school. Where is everyone?" They listened sympathetically, but there wasn't anything that they could do either because none of the others had arrived yet.

Shortly afterwards, three or four people arrived and we were ushered into a conference room. My lawyer never showed up, and I couldn't understand what was being said nor could I read any of the papers they handed me to sign. I had never signed a legal paper in my life before my lawyer had advised me to do so, but this time I did. There was no one to advise me and I didn't want to be offensive or lose the flat by refusing to sign the contract before my lawyer had read it. After the papers were signed the lawyer representing the owners asked me for the deposit, which was in the form of a banker's draft. My masquerade of calm and control vanished the second they asked for money. The girl's father was the only one who realized how frightened I was. He asked them to bring me a glass of water. My mouth was so dry I could barely speak. I told him, "I thought your lawyer would hold the deposit in an escrow account until everything was settled and you turned over the deed of the property to me."

He said, "No, this is only the deposit, saying you will complete the sale. Don't worry, it's alright. That's the way it's done here." So I handed his daughter the cheque made out in her name for cash, and got up to leave for Nicky's school.

My family had taught me to rely on lawyers, so I was lost when mine hadn't shown up. I didn't know what I had signed and all sorts of fears raced through my head. There were always stories in the news about some damn fool like me being tricked out of large sums of money. I wondered how people could be so naïve. And there was I, signing everything, potentially placing myself in the same situation, so as not to appear offensive. From somewhere deep in my subconscious, I heard my grandfather's voice castigating me. Dearly departed, but I felt his presence as if he had slipped unnoticed in to the room. "Always use the best lawyer," he said. He was forever going on about lawyers, and now everything he told me came flooding back into my consciousness. Once when I was a child he took me around his property and showed me a narrow strip of land he had been awarded in a lawsuit against his neighbour. It wasn't much wider than the hedge, but he was delighted to have won. He attributed this windfall to the genius of his lawyer, and we walked up and down admiring the tiny strip together. I was young, maybe seven or eight years old, impressionable. He told me then, "Remember, always hire the best lawyer. Sometime in the future you will need one." I listened; taking everything in. He was adamant that I should know.

Grandpa loomed larger than life. He was rich, powerful, and eccentric; at least in my mind. He never fussed over me. I was a girl, and although I was an offspring of my mother who he dearly loved, she had already produced the son and heir he had longed for, relegating me to nothing special. So this unexpected concern and advice to me alone made a big impression. I wasn't sure if my lawyer was any good. He was recommended by friends, but he hadn't shown up, so he probably didn't count. My grandfather's voice came back telling me, "Never sign anything before you've read it." Everything he had ever told me about lawyers came flooding back. I felt weak. I could still feel him holding my hand, cautioning me just as he had done when I was a child. He had tried to protect me and probably just for this occasion. Now I was lost. I waited for my mother's voice asking: "You just signed what!?!"

My brain was bombarded with doubts. All the fear and insecurity I had been able to suppress came out and attacked me, until the memory of my grandmother took me away from the present. She often told me: "Darling, the world is your oyster," believing the world was mine to enjoy. Later I realized that she hadn't understood the script, and had missed an essential part of its meaning. She didn't share grandpa's infatuation with lawyers. Her advice was always the same: "Never compromise your integrity," "Don't drink out of a bottle," and, "Use the right stationery." "If you play around with convention, first make sure you have mastered the rules." For her, manners were a form of identification. "People know who you are by how you behave, and they treat you accordingly, unless of course they are savages and then, for goodness sake, you have no business associating with them." I believed in manners too, but I would have been much happier if my lawyer had shown up. Now it was too late. The papers were signed. They had the cheque, and they were leaving the room.

I battled my way through these voices, all of which had shaped my life, but none of them were mine. I could not separate and find myself amidst the confusion of other people's values and beliefs. Their advice had taken over, filling the space where I should have been; making me afraid to decide anything on my own. Only when I moved to Peru was I forced to make my own decisions, and I wasn't ready.

Half way to Nicky's school I panicked. I had no idea what I had signed, nor if it had been right to hand over the deposit. It was Mother's Day and I couldn't arrive at Nicky's school in this state, but I couldn't be late. In my broken Spanish, I begged the driver to pull over and find a pay phone so that I could ring a friend, and I told him everything that had happened at the notary's office. He said, "Relax gringa," and reassured me over and over again that everything was alright. But nothing felt right. It was a big accomplishment for me to go to the shop alone, so buying a flat all by myself was quite overwhelming. Then my positive voice came in and told me, "The owners seemed like such nice people."

I arrived at Nicky's school just in time to be lined up with the rest of the contestants in the Mothers' Egg Race. There wasn't time to catch my breath or to protest before someone had shoved the handle of a spoon in my mouth, balancing what was, hopefully, a hardboiled egg on the other end. Nicky was sitting on the sidelines with his classmates. He looked over at me, relieved that I was there, but at the same time mortified that his mother had been the one chosen to represent his house and all his new friends. When the whistle blew I shot out ahead of the other mothers, determined to make him proud by winning the race.

MOVING TO THE NEW FLAT!

The first thing I bought to furnish the new flat was an antique brass bed for Nicky's room. I bought it from a friend of a friend who was selling a few things, and Giannina accompanied me to take a look. Part of the sales agreement was that the vendor would arrange to have the bed delivered, which he did the next day. The men arrived on time, and didn't complain when they discovered our lift was so tiny that they would have to carry the heavy metal frame up four flights of steps. They were also diligent about protecting both the bed and the walls on the way up, so we hired them to come back and move us to the new flat.

When the movers returned the following week, Gloria asked the Porter to open the garage door so they could load the truck off the main road. We waited inside to show them my parking space. As the garage door swung open the driver revved the engine of his dilapidated truck to bursting point, in order to get it up and over the threshold. He shot in, filling the air with a dense cloud of smoke. The Porter was sympathetic, but annoyed that he had allowed them in. Between the noise and the fumes, one of the tenants was sure to complain, and he would bear the brunt of their anger. The pickup truck was pockmarked with rust and held together mostly by wire and duct tape. Its tires hadn't a shadow of tread. Crowded in the back were family members who had come along to help.

Seeing the condition of the truck, I told Gloria: "Tell them I will pay them for coming and any expenses, but to go home. Say the Señora has changed her mind about moving today." But she refused. They were waiting for my instructions, and she didn't have the heart to send them away.

My Spanish had hardly advanced far enough to ask them their names, so without her help I wasn't able to ask them to leave. The men eagerly started packing and the truck was loaded before I realized that they hadn't brought boxes or newspaper to wrap up and protect our belongings. Everything had been put into the plastic carrier bags they had found in our kitchen! Then they piled all of the bags on the floor of the truck, and the family climbed in, securing the bags with their hands and feet. When they set off we waved goodbye. Everything we owned in Lima was riding in the back of that truck, and I smiled to myself, wondering if I would see either them or any of our clothes again.

We followed a few minutes later and found the truck waiting outside our building. The truck's occupants already looked like the Peruvian Beverly Hillbillies, sitting there in their battered pickup, and we only added to the illusion by pulling up behind them in a local cab. The Porter hadn't allowed them to bring anything inside or unload. He eyed me with uncertainty as I approached the front door, waving my new keys as our only form of identification. I realized at once I had dressed too informally for the move; first impressions are important. The Porter, brushed and polished, stood proud and erect in his stiff navy uniform. He didn't hide his disdain for my motley crew, or for Spot, who was obliged to take the service lift with the movers while Nicky and I rode up alone in the main lift.

Ours was an imposing modern building, with a certain cachet. I'm sure that the other owners would have arrived there with their architects and decorators, to customise their space first, before moving in. Only after their apartments had been gutted, new cabinetry installed, walls painted, and rooms decorated, would truckloads of furniture and boxes of personal belongings then arrive and be unloaded by scores of uniformed men from a well-known moving company. Our flat was several thousand square feet, but the only piece of furniture we brought was an antique bed frame, minus the mattress, plus a few suitcases. Everything else was stuffed into plastic carrier bags.

The Porter was disappointed when he realized we were the new owners. We clearly brought down the tone of the place. I imagined my father commiserating with him: "Uh oh, there goes the neighbourhood!"

After our few belongings were brought up, we paid the movers and they left. That was the first time Nicky and I were alone in the flat. Armandina had taken a shower and gone home. Gloria, our live-in-maid-cum-nanny, stayed at the rental flat to clean and to make sure we hadn't left anything behind. Salvador came by for a few minutes to see how things were going, but when he saw the chaos he left. I only saw Salvador a couple of days a week, at best, so I wasn't surprised to see him leave so quickly. Ours wasn't the type of romance that made us in any way inseparable, and he knew I wouldn't invite him to stay.

Soon after Salvador left, Nicky and I heard water running and I went to investigate. I didn't see any water, so I just assumed our plumbing was poorly insulated. Nicky was in his bedroom arranging his toys, and I started unpacking our clothes. I forgot all about the water until I went to the kitchen and saw it streaming across the dining room floor and out over the balcony. I raced back through the kitchen and into the laundry room where I found water pouring out from under the water heater. A pipe had burst, and water was spraying everywhere, including in the direction of the electrical switch that should turn off the water heater.

I used a broom handle to flip off the electricity and put our only bucket under the broken pipe, but there was far too much water to contain. I shouted for Nicky to come, and begged him to help by going down to tell the Porter, but he didn't know the Porter so he wouldn't budge. In the meantime, I kept running to the sink to empty the bucket, and started silently crying.

Our building had only one flat per floor and the elevator opened directly into each flat, so we couldn't run next door for help. In any case, we had only been there for a few hours; I didn't know our neighbours, nor if they spoke English. On top of that, my white shirt was soaked through and had become transparent. I was too embarrassed to meet anyone. To add to my distress, we had no insurance for the flat, it had been too complicated for me to arrange on my own.

Water was now everywhere, and more was coming out, so in desperation I ran to the intercom and tried ringing the Porter. After pushing all the buttons on the intercom, a person answered, it might have been the porter, and I pleaded: "Help! Please! Flood! Please help me!" Whoever answered said some equally alien words back in Spanish, so neither of us understood the other.

It was a waste of time talking, and I ran back to the broken pipe. This time I found the stopcock and turned off all the water, but the damage was done. Water was pouring under the door of the service lift and down the back staircase; gallons and gallons of water. I was terrified my neighbours would follow the water up the steps to my door and, once they had found the source, would bang on the door berating me in a language I couldn't understand. I also worried about what else might go wrong, or that perhaps that all of the plumbing was a mess. I had no idea. I hadn't done a survey on the flat, and I didn't even know a plumber.

I discovered the phone number of the father of the previous owner, which by some miracle he had given me when we exchanged contracts, telling me if there was anything I needed to ring them. I didn't know if I would be able to reach him or if he would help. The money for the flat had been exchanged, we were now the owners, it was our problem; but he had seemed so kind and he was the only one who would know how to reach their plumber. So I steeled myself for rejection and rang him. It was late, but he came over straight away and took charge of everything, including ringing the Porter, who found people to come and mop up the water. Our first hours in the building could have been a disaster, but instead we were overwhelmed by everyone's kindness. They were apologetic that we should have suffered such a terrible experience on our first day; several of the maintenance men stayed late to help.

Like almost everything else in our lives during that time, the entrance hadn't gone according to plan. But it was a blessing in disguise because we met everyone working in the building and they became very protective of us.

TROUBLE AT SCHOOL

Nothing escaped Nicky's curiosity, and he never accepted anything without an explanation. Which didn't go down well at school. When he began kindergarten, Peter and I wanted him to have a fresh start, and let his teachers form their own opinions. It was only a matter of weeks before they called me in for a meeting. Peter was in London so I went on my own. One teacher told me: "Nicky turns the tables on their side, creating makeshift fortresses and barricades, which is creative. The problem is, he won't let other children play on the tables he is building with. He wanders out of class and disappears if we are not watching him every second."

In London, Nicky was often getting into trouble. Just before we left, Santa Claus arrived at Nicky's school and he walked over to Santa and ripped off his beard, saying: "Look, he's a fake!" Some of the children cried and Santa Claus wanted to leave. Nicky was taken upstairs to the Head's office. When I arrived he said, "Mummy I was just showing them that Santa Claus wasn't real." I wasn't sure how to react when she explained to me about the beard. Santa Claus wasn't real, nor did he look real, and Nicky hadn't pulled the beard off to be cruel, so I couldn't understand why he wasn't quietly taken aside and praised for his observation. Children who are bold enough to speak out when they see something that isn't right shouldn't be punished. We left his school hand-in-hand, in disgrace. Nicky couldn't understand what he had done wrong and I wasn't about to tell him, "People don't always want to hear the truth. Sometimes you have to go along with a lie to keep out of trouble."

In order to appease the new school, I agreed to take Nicky to a therapist who worked with gifted children. She would, "Teach him to put his energy to good use, rather than get into trouble." Nicky met with her twice a week, and they talked and played games. Sometimes she would ask me to stay so that she could observe us together. Nicky was asked to initiate the games, and once he chose a doll's house for us to play with. I am at a total loss with imaginary games. Board games are fun, and I enjoy making up stories, but in any case, it's hard to be creative while someone is watching and taking notes.

Nicky started by arranging the furniture inside the doll's house. When I tried to join in he told me: "No! I want to do it by myself," which was fine with me. All the while I was discreetly looking at my watch, willing the hour to be over. As soon as everything was set up, Nicky handed me the sitting figure of a boy to play with. It wasn't designed for running. Its legs were moulded for a chair, permanently bent. I felt like an idiot when Nicky suddenly shot across the table with his running figure and expected mine to chase him.

The therapist was off to the side, taking notes. I wanted to be a good sport and play along with the game, so changing my voice to sound like a craggy old lady, I told Nicky: "Wait, slow down, my legs are stiff. Give me a moment to straighten up." Then in a provocative voice I told him: "I'm coming to get you," and, holding my figure with the bent paralyzed legs, I chased his figure around the set.

The next moment Nicky changed the game. The doll's house began shaking, simulating an earthquake, which are common in Peru. People and furniture were falling over and scattering in all directions. Before then I felt awkward wondering what to do. Now at least our session was entertaining. Meanwhile the therapist was feverishly scribbling notes.

Seconds later Nicky turned the house upside down and he put the entire family, along with the bathroom fixtures, on what had then become the roof. Most of the family were swept away by an aeroplane he had found on the desk. Only the sitting grandmother figure, which had helplessly fallen over, still remained. There was no escape for Grandma! He picked her up and plonked her on the toilet, which was now on the roof, and started making noises as if she were trying to defecate. I carried on playing with a straight face.

At the end of the session, the therapist turned towards Nicky and, in a voice straining to sound nonchalant, she said, "Do you want to hurt your family?"

He looked at her, and then turned to me and asked: "Mummy, is she crazy?"

I never learned to play, but I learned that even though I had been physically "there" for Nicky twenty-four hours a day, I had been distant because of my own problems. Slowly, after many sessions, the therapist showed me that he had included me in his drawings again.

NOT SPEAKING THE LANGUAGE

It never occurred to me before moving to Lima that not speaking Spanish would be such a handicap, nor did I realize how difficult or necessary it would be for me to learn the language. My friends spoke English, but the majority of people in Peru didn't, which caused me to be dependent on friends. I found it difficult to socialize at parties. I couldn't express myself intelligently, nor could I follow what people were saying. Both of which stripped me of a personality.

I am neither glamorous nor charismatic enough for people to gravitate to me when I enter a room. I need to make an effort to meet people. I have been described as handsome, and it has been said that I look well bred, but I have often found that that is a polite way of saying the woman they are describing is plain. Handsome doesn't conjure up the vision of a woman slinking into the room in stiletto heels and oozing sexuality, but of someone you might safely take home to meet your mother. I needed to captivate and amuse, but instead I looked bored. I went to parties and listened to people laughing, watching their animated expressions as they told stories. I stayed hour after hour, trying to look interested and amused but never understanding what they were saying. It felt as though a physical barrier had been erected between us. The words were meaningless sounds that communicated nothing to me, and I became conscious of the loneliness and isolation one would feel being deaf. I sank into another world at parties, entertaining myself with random thoughts and articles I had read. Whiskey helped, because after a few glasses I appeared to be enjoying myself and I probably was. I no longer cared what was being said, and became uninhibited about interrupting conversations with something totally irrelevant. No one got annoyed; it reminded them I was there and they would switch back to English for a moment, pulling me back into the conversation.

In the beginning people would ask, "What are you doing here? Why did you move to Peru?" Which hurt my feelings - it felt as if they were saying, "What are you doing here? You don't belong!" However, in truth, it was my own fear that I didn't belong or fit in, and sometimes I wondered even more than they did what we were doing in Lima. It wasn't until after we had lived there for some time that I really understood why they were curious. At first, I was too wrapped up in getting Nicky adjusted to a new school and settling in to notice how few foreigners there were in our group of friends. We were certainly the only foreigners I knew living there without any specific reason. I wasn't there because of work. I didn't have a Peruvian husband or come because of a lover. I hardly met any foreigners in Lima; except those with the embassies and a few people who were sent there by companies. I had moved to Peru with no other explanation than because I wanted to, which sounded a bit impetuous. But it sounded less bizarre than responding: "Because it was predestined."

It had been easy for me to fit in when we moved to England all those years ago. I was young, I spoke the language, and I was in school, where it was simple to make friends. The only frustration I had in London was that even after living there for half my life I still sounded like a tourist. I got sick of hearing, "Well, you certainly haven't lost your accent," or, "Are you here on holiday?" No matter how long we stayed in Lima, I knew I would never sound Peruvian; and worse, I worried that I would never speak the language well enough to be understood.

Everyone we knew in Lima belonged there. They were part of a small, closely-knit society, and Nicky and I were total outsiders. But we were never left out. I was taken along to weddings, wakes, births, and with friends to visit their family in hospital, people that I had never met before. I was only excluded by my own inability to learn Spanish. The few foreigners I knew in Lima had long since been absorbed into Peruvian society through marriage or the length of time they had been there, and they spoke the language. By the time I recognized we did look a little out of place, everyone had gotten used to us and had stopped asking me why we were there.

By then I felt as if we belonged in Peru and I had stopped asking myself that same question.

RUNOFF ELECTION –
28TH MAY 2000

Preparations began in earnest for the runoff election which was required since none of the candidates had gained the 50 percent majority necessary to win outright. However, before the runoff could take place, Toledo dropped out of the race and called for a boycott as a protest against voting irregularities. This left one party running, effectively assuring that Fujimori would remain in power. Despite that, he was still running for a third term, which many considered unconstitutional. Thousands of irregularities came into question. There were talks of postponing the election to give more time to mediate a solution with Toledo and get him back into the race, and to investigate charges of vote tampering. There was evidence that campaign workers had forged signatures to get Fujimori on the ballot, and that the leading opposition candidate's name had been cut from many of the voting sheets.

Peru keeps strict records of all eligible voters. However, when the votes were tallied from the election, the numbers exceeded the eligible voters by one million votes. The Oficina Nacional de Procesos Electorales - ONPE - gave no explanation for the discrepancy.

Fujimori ignored the recommendations proposed by the national and international observers to establish fairness and credibility for the election. Instead his campaign grew more reckless. He controlled most of what aired on the news, and he launched a major smear campaign against Toledo, suggesting that Toledo was a mentally unstable womanizer; and a heavy drinker who also took drugs. The opposition didn't appear to have a voice on television, so Toledo withdrew rather than lending credibility to a sham election. The monitors from The Organization of American States also withdrew, charging that, under the circumstances, it was unlikely to be an impartial election. Toledo encouraged his supporters to deface their ballots, writing: "No to fraud," and thereby invalidating their votes.

It was no surprise when Fujimori remained president. Most everyone I spoke to was resigned to the fact he would be president again. Fujimori was a hero to many; he was admired for ending terrorism, stopping hyperinflation, and opening up the economy. He had succeeded against all the odds in ending terrorism, which his predecessors had failed to do. Dramatic measures were needed and executed to end terrorism; fighting fire with fire, doing whatever it took to make things better for Peru. When all was said and done, he was "the devil they knew."

During his previous terms as president Fujimori's popularity was volatile, and his handling of a siege at the Japanese Residence in 1997 attracted negative worldwide attention. One of his major achievements as president was ridding the country of terrorism. There were still small isolated groups hiding in remote areas, but their leaders were in jail and with no one to unite them they were no longer considered a significant threat. However, the organized precision of the Japanese embassy attack caused people to lose confidence that terrorism was truly over. The siege began when a group from the Túpac Amaru Revolutionary Movement got past armed police and bodyguards by blasting a hole through the garden wall, capturing hundreds of dignitaries celebrating Emperor Akihito's birthday. Once inside they gained the advantage, because the building was so fortified that, even with their small group, it was easy to defend. Most of the hostages other than those connected to the government were eventually released. Fourteen terrorists held captive the remaining seventy-two men.

After 126 days Fujimori sent in commandos, killing the terrorists inside. At first, he was hailed as a hero for rescuing the hostages. There was little sympathy for the fourteen rebels killed, but later reliable witnesses testified that some of the terrorists had surrendered. According to reports, Fujimori gave the order to: "Take no MRTA alive," causing concern that the terrorists were executed. When Fujimori first came to power Peru was near the top of worldwide ratings for terrorist attacks. Sendero Luminoso - the Shining Path - had plagued Peru for more than a decade, murdering tens of thousands of innocent people, including priests, trade union organizers, farmers, and students. Fujimori bent all the rules while in office, which was generally tolerated at first because he ended terrorism and brought the economy up, but once equilibrium was restored his methods could no longer be excused.

The word "fraud" popped into every conversation. Even many of Fujimori's most ardent supporters admitted that the election was corrupt, but it was expected. They felt Fujimori had done a good job when Peru was at its lowest ebb. Toledo and Fujimori had much in common; they were both academically gifted, both studied in the States, and more notable, neither candidate was part of the oligarchy or of Spanish or other European descent. They had risen to the top politically, but with little political experience and as complete outsiders. Toledo was virtually unknown until he was thrust into the limelight as leader of the opposition against

Fujimori in this controversial election. He had been a minister of labour under President Belaúnde, and chief economic adviser to the Central Bank of Peru, but he lacked political experience, and no one knew if he had it in him to be president.

During the United States presidential election in 2000 I invited a few Peruvian friends over for drinks and canapés to watch the results come in. Having gone to so many election parties in Lima, I thought it would be fun to invite the same group over to watch my election. However, instead of the well-ordered and squeaky-clean election that we had all expected, this one took a subtle detour. At first they announced that Al Gore was in the lead, and the press prematurely declared him a winner. Afterwards they changed their message and decided that it was too close to call. Then George Bush went into the lead, and all hell broke loose. As we drank Pisco Sours we joked that the situation was reminiscent of the last vote count in Peru. The following day angry crowds dominated the news, openly shouting fraud and protesting in the street, this time in the United States. My friends teased me saying, "Hey gringa, your elections don't seem all that dissimilar to ours. Except with that amount of irregularities we would be vilified, and forced by the international community into another election."

Later they joked, "How does it work that the Supreme Court decided the election? Aren't they nominated by the president? Sounds suspicious!"

PROTEST AGAINST SWEARING IN OF FUJIMORI

Despite all the controversy surrounding his election, on 29th July 2000, amidst rioting, tear gas, 40,000 riot police, thousands of protesters, fires burning out of control and six people dead, Fujimori was sworn in for his third term as President of Peru.

Toledo encouraged his supporters to take part in a peaceful demonstration directed towards Congress, as a protest against "the massive irregularities, and to prevent the inauguration." The protest got out of control. The streets in the centre of Lima became a battlefield between protesters and the police. Riot police fired tear gas, and water cannons were used to hold back the thousands of protesters. It was later rumoured that agents provocateurs were sent from the NIS, the National Intelligence Service, to cause chaos and to destroy property; that they were the ones who started the fire in a bank in which six security guards died, making it look as if Toledo was the one inciting violence and that his followers were out of control. Toledo was initially blamed for the murders, and there were calls out to arrest him, but instead of running away Toledo came forward and accused infiltrators sent by the NIS of starting the bank fire. Which sounded more credible; and, with suspicion aroused, Fujimori backed down on his accusations.

After the elections the government was dealt another blow when one of Montesinos' secret videos, recorded with hidden cameras, was stolen and leaked on television by Channel N. It showed him bribing an opposition congressman to switch sides in order to bring up Fujimori's numbers in Congress. The tapes eventually led to the arrests of many important people. Other charges against Montesinos included human rights violations, arms deals, drug trafficking and arranging death squads, but it wasn't until the film became public that Fujimori fired Montesinos. Fujimori also agreed to step down and have new elections, promising he wouldn't run. After he fired Montesinos there were rumours of a coup. Montesinos had strong ties with the military and there were fears he wouldn't leave without a fight; but the military supported Fujimori's call for new elections.

During his time in office Montesinos amassed a vast collection of secretly recorded videos showing people in positions of power accepting cash for favors; others were set up in a brothel and filmed cavorting with prostitutes. He used these videos as protection, and for extorting favors. After the brothel tapes were released, the court considered them too intimate to use as evidence; and the delicate task of returning them to the victims, if they wanted them, was entrusted to the Catholic Bishops. Later thousands of the "Vladivideos" - as they became known - were recovered; but few were ever shown to the public.

After the video scandal was made public, Montesinos fled to Panama to avoid arrest. He was denied political asylum because of the charges of human rights violations against him, but he was allowed in on a tourist visa. Many Panamanians opposed granting Montesinos asylum. One protester held up a sign saying: "We Are

Not the Garbage Can of the World." Panama, which was known to allow refuge to other reprehensible leaders, drew the line at Montesinos.

A month later Montesinos flew back to Peru through an air force controlled base and disappeared. Fujimori, who claimed to know nothing of his whereabouts, led a melodramatic search for him flanked by the press, which seemed bizarre at the time. Later it was realized that it wasn't Montesinos he was looking for, but the videos. He wanted to remove any that were incriminating for him. A few days later, Montesinos escaped to Venezuela on a private yacht, seeking political asylum and the protection of President Chavez. Eight months later he was captured and deported back to Peru.

The media kept unravelling more and more scandals inside and outside of the government.

13TH NOVEMBER 2000 - GONE TO BRUNEI

Fujimori's third term in office ended sooner than anyone could have imagined. Within months of his re-election he left for the Asian-Pacific Economic Cooperation in Brunei, and, amid all the scandals breaking out over Montesinos, he never returned to Peru. Fujimori faxed his resignation from Tokyo, but rather than accepting his resignation Congress declared him "morally unfit to rule" in order to remove him by impeachment. The Peruvian Supreme Court then issued an international arrest warrant for Fujimori, alleging that he was involved with massacres in which 25 people died.

Because Fujimori was a dual national Japan would not extradite him, and Peru's legal system does not allow trials in absentia, so as long as Fujimori stayed in Japan he was safe from prosecution. Paniagua became the interim president, and freedom of the press was restored.

Peru also returned to the jurisdiction of the Inter-American Court of Human Rights. Even if most of what was going on around me went over my head, it was an extraordinary time to have taken up residence in Peru.

MOM ARRIVES FOR A VISIT

Nicky and I had only been living in Lima for a few months when my mother decided to come and visit. The flat was sparsely furnished; all we had were a few pieces of furniture that I had bought from the previous owners. There was no furniture in her bedroom other than a couple of chairs and a bed I had bought when she told me she was coming. None of our furniture or household things were due to arrive from London for another few months. But we had everything we needed. I filled the huge terracotta pots on the balconies to overflowing with red geraniums and two enormous cacti, which I bought from a man selling off a cart in the street below. The southwest side of the drawing room was glass; on a clear day, we could see the coast, and in the evening we had panoramic views of the sunsets.

I was enrolled to start Spanish for beginners; the class was a couple of hours a day, and I suggested to my mother that she might want to take the course with me. The school wasn't far. We could walk there and be home in time for lunch. Mummy and I were the oldest students in Spanish One; the rest were mostly in their teens and twenties. They were quick to learn and lots of fun. We studied hard, but even in Beginners Spanish we struggled, especially with the complicated verbs and conjugations. It was difficult for us to keep up, and on the last day of class, we were reminded that we had an exam the next day. I was miserable, because very likely I wouldn't pass and move on with the rest of the class to the next level. I would be stuck for another month in Spanish One, alone. Mom was excused the exam because she was leaving for the States.

I was agonising over the exam, and pouring out my frustration on the walk home. We didn't notice the man following us until he grabbed the strap of my handbag with both his hands, pulling down hard, trying to break the strap on my shoulder. At first I thought he was angry because we were walking so slowly and blocking his way. It didn't occur to me that he wanted to rob me. I turned toward him, our faces inches apart, and snapped: "What is your problem?" It wasn't until I hit the ground that I realized I was in trouble.

My immediate reaction was indignation, and then determination not to let go. The thief wasn't any larger or stronger than me, maybe younger, but I had an equal advantage of strength because I was enraged and surging with adrenalin. What I hadn't realized was that he worked with an accomplice, and they were well-practiced at robbing pedestrians. Their system was for one person to grab the handbag while his partner pulled alongside in a car. Whereupon the thief would dive into the vehicle through the open passenger window, clutching the handbag as the car sped away. Normally they were gone in seconds.

I was still gripping the strap of the handbag when the car drove away. My mother was screaming and I could feel the sting of the pavement burning my hand and legs. I couldn't let go of the strap, my hand had frozen shut, and when I looked up I saw the thief dangling from the car window above me and I felt his shoe against my face. At that same moment, I became conscious that I was being hurt, maybe badly hurt, and I started to wet my pants. There were people running after the car shouting, trying to reach me. I was mortified that they were going to see me dripping wet, so I focused all my strength on clenching my pelvic muscles, struggling to stop the flow, which wasn't easy considering the circumstances. In seconds everything stopped moving and people surrounded me, mostly gardeners and porters who had run after the car to help. They picked me up and I held the handbag above my head. I didn't feel triumphant. It was more of a gesture to show everyone I was all right. Afterward, someone brought me my shoes and my other things that had been scattered down the road. I heard her voice and turned back to see my mother. She hadn't moved, which allowed me to gauge the distance I had been dragged. She kept repeating: "Muffi why didn't you let go of the handbag? Why didn't you just let go?" I spoke but my voice faltered. I became her child again and whispered back, "Mummy they hurt me. Look they really hurt me," which only made her more distressed. One of the porters took us inside his building while someone hailed us a cab. As we were leaving he handed me a slip of paper with the licence number of the car they had used in the mugging.

We got into the cab and made our way home. My wrist had been scraped to the bone, and my hip was bleeding through my shredded clothes. Peter and Nicky were in my bedroom when we arrived. Nicky saw me, but he seemed far more concerned for me that I had started to wet my pants rather than that I had returned covered with blood. Peter rang the police, but they told him they couldn't accept a statement over the phone and that he would have to go to the police station if he wanted to file a report. Peter explained to me that reporting it was a waste of time, but I was too fired up with adrenalin and emotion to let it go. I wanted justice. After more than an hour, Peter returned home from the police station and told me that I had been given a Court Order to see a police doctor, which was standard procedure, and that it would be best for us to go now and get it out of the way. He was returning to

London in a couple of days and the officer had told him that the doctor's office was open until five o'clock, so after changing my clothes and loosely bandaging my wounds we left for the centre of Lima.

What the police officer hadn't told Peter was that we were required to pay for the doctor's visit, and that could only be done at a certain bank, which had different hours. It closed earlier than the clinic. We didn't have a receipt showing that we had paid, so the guard turned us away. I argued with the guard, but he didn't understand. Peter warned me: "Muffi for heaven's sake shut up." When we returned home, I went to look for my mother. I wanted to make a joke about our experience and to see how she was. Armandina told me she was in the kitchen so I went there to find her.

She hadn't noticed me enter and I watched my mother, who is normally invincible, trembling, and unable to pour herself a drink. I felt guilty to be there like an intruder spying on her, but at the same time I was afraid to move for fear of startling her again. Her hands were shaking and water was splashing out over the top of her cup. I remained frozen in the doorway, watching her until she saw me. Neither of us spoke. We didn't need to. I already knew what she was thinking by the expression on her face. Normally she didn't interfere with our lives, she kept her feelings to herself, but this time her emotions overwhelmed her and she let slip: "Muffi I thought you were going to die. I thought I was going to lose you." That was the end of the conversation.

Peter took me to the police doctor the following day. This time the bank was open, so we paid and got the receipt that would allow us to go inside and see the doctor, whose office was situated in the Palace of Justice, El Palacio de Justicia, which was inspired in its design by the Palace of Justice in Brussels. It is smaller in scale and minus the dome; nonetheless, it is an imposing Neo-Classical building. We climbed the mountain of steps framed by columns, griffins and lions that lead you to the entrance. We made it to the top, but before we could reach the elaborate brass doors to enter we were intercepted by security men and directed to a less impressive staircase, this time leading to our door, in the basement. When we entered the building, I said to Peter, "You must be joking! I'm leaving. If this were a veterinarian's office I would take our dog home." He retorted, "You have a court order to see the doctor: I warned you not to report the mugging. I don't want to be here. I am here as a favour to you. Leave if you want, but then you'll have to sort it out on your own." Faced with this ultimatum, I followed him in.

Peter handed the guard the receipt, and he barred Peter from entering: "No, not you. You can't go in without a paper. Wait in the hall. She has to see the doctor on her own." When Peter told me this I demanded a translator. I said to the guard in English, "I have a court order to be here because I sure as hell wouldn't be here for any other reason. If the court is forcing me to see one of their doctors they are going to have to provide a translator." The policeman looked blank and talked to Peter again, at length. Then, he nodded sympathetically to Peter and let him in.

The waiting room was packed with people sitting on stark wooden benches, tightly lined up in rows. Most of the people there looked far more battered than me. We were the only foreigners. I asked Peter: "Don't they have another place for tourists? Why can't I go to see my own doctor?" Getting mugged was one thing but being there was too much. I had already made a mental note not to report it to the police if I was mugged again.

We waited for what seemed an eternity. Peter and I got into another argument while everyone else sat in nervous silence. I wanted to leave and told Peter, "We don't belong here. I want to go to Giannina's doctor." I had open wounds on my hands and feet, and I told Peter, "Come on, let's leave, we've been here long enough. This place isn't sanitary. If I stay any longer I am going to die from an infection." Every time we raised our voices a sea of shiny black hair turned in unison, exposing worried faces. When we stopped arguing they breathed a sigh of relief and turned back to facing the wall of doors and waiting their turn for the next doctor. Many of the people there were victims of domestic violence and they wanted to be sure to get out of the way if Peter and I got into a fight and started hurtling benches at each other. After an hour, or more, we were called in to see one of the doctors. He was in a small windowless cubicle, more like a cell. Not quite like Harley Street or any other doctor's office I had ever visited.

I declined to sit on one of the chairs he offered. I wanted to skip the formalities and leave as quickly as possible. He asked to see my wounds, and I closed the door with my foot so as not to touch it, and dropped my trousers to show him the road burns on my hip and legs. Peter did all of the talking, which he does especially when he is nervous. He talked non-stop, which appeared to be welcome entertainment for the doctor, who normally sat there all day seeing patients, filling out forms, writing such things as raped, stabbed, concussion, hit and run, and worse. Usually when the consultation was over he mechanically shouted: "Next." Instead he talked with Peter, and chuckled. Peter was in good form, making amends for me who, with my dreadful Spanish and uncooperative nature, was proving to be awkward.

When our meeting was over, the doctor stood up and shook hands with Peter. They leaned forward in a partial embrace and with their free hands they slapped each other heartily on the back, which Latin men do as a sign of camaraderie or friendship. He handed Peter a paper and explained: "Now you need to take the report to another office in the building to file it." Peter accompanied me to the next room, and when they finished the paperwork a man came in and fingerprinted me. I examined my black fingertips in disbelief, and when he noticed the expression on my face, thinking I wanted a tissue he told me: "Sorry, we don't have any paper." The clerk apologetically told Peter they didn't have any tissue in the bathroom either, not that I would have considered going in there for any reason.

I told the man, "In other countries, they fingerprint the criminals, not the victims!" When I spoke like this it drove Peter crazy. So I said it again. Peter cautioned me: "Keep quiet or you will get us both into trouble." But I could no longer stay quiet. It was obvious from their looks they didn't understand me, but I needed to speak. I was also annoyed that Peter had to interpret and I didn't trust what he was saying. I knew just enough Spanish to know that he wasn't translating what I was asking him to say, but I couldn't speak for myself, and it was no use arguing with him.

Peter told me later he explained my outburst to the man by saying, "My wife is still hysterical from the mugging, but she passionately wanted to express, in her own words, her gratitude for all your help and to thank you personally for the attention she has received. She is thanking you from her heart and wishes to tell you: Long live the Lima police force and may God protect all of you and your families in your gallant never ending battle for justice!"

Peter handed the police the paper that the Porter had given me with the number and description of the car that the robbers used. In return, the police showed us a file with details of the same car being reported, with the same number plate robbing other pedestrians on the same street. That wasn't encouraging, especially as most people in Lima don't usually report muggings unless their identity cards or cellular phones are taken. Peter quickly pulled me out of the office before I had time to comment on that little revelation.

By the time Salvador rang to ask how I was, Peter was back in London. He had called to remind me we had a date for a party the following evening, and asked if I still wanted to go. I told him, "Yes. It will be nice to see you."

We arrived early, almost the first, and secured a good table. The party was in the garden of one of the embassies and after dinner there was dancing to a live band. The evening was fabulous, but our date was a disaster from the start. Salvador parked several blocks from the embassy and we walked, which we had often done, but this time I was frightened to be out on the street. I felt vulnerable wearing a large diamond broach I had inherited from my grandmother, and was terrified that at any second I would be knocked down and robbed. I clung to Salvador's arm and only relaxed my grip when we passed through the gate of the embassy where there were guards with machine guns to protect us. After being mugged, I had changed from the more confident, devil-may-care woman that he had first met, to someone clingy and insecure. He found my vulnerability suffocating. That night I knew our relationship had ended. The timing was wrong. Just when I needed someone to be there, I was back on my own.

A man I had met on many occasions came over when he saw me standing alone, and asked: "Is everything alright? You seem lost."

I told him, "I'm fine. I was mugged last week and I'm still a little jittery to be out in public."

He replied, "You're lucky you're in one piece. Wait until you have lived here for a while. You'll hear some real horror stories about muggings and kidnappings."

Before I had a chance to ask him what he meant, his group returned and whisked him away. I tried not to appear desperate as I wove in and out through the crowd of unfamiliar faces, frantically searching for Salvador or anyone else I might recognize, in the hope that they might take me home.

SPOT STOLEN

We didn't dwell on the mugging, nor did we talk about it, but I was still traumatized and couldn't sleep. On Friday, at around five o'clock, I went to kiss my mother goodnight. I wanted to have an early night, but Nicky and the nanny hadn't returned from walking Spot, so I watched the news with her while waiting for them to return home. Suddenly, the door burst open and they were rushing in. Nicky was hysterical; the nanny was crying. They were incoherent. We couldn't understand what was wrong. All I knew was that Nicky was safe in my arms. Then, to my horror, I realized that Spot wasn't with them. I asked, "Where is Spot?" They both answered at once, and neither of them were making sense. All I knew was that we had to find Spot and bring him home.

I left Nicky with my mother while the nanny and I ran out to look for him. She told me that while they were walking home two young men came over pretending to admire Spot, and they squatted down to pet him. People often came over to look at Spot and to stroke him. Pugs are curious looking animals and they were rare in Lima at the time, so he attracted all sorts of attention. At times drivers stopped their car in the road to take a closer look. But while the thieves were petting Spot, they were also unclipping his leash. They grabbed him by the harness, and, using it like a handle, they lifted him off the ground and ran away. Nicky and the nanny tried to catch them, but Nicky was too small to keep up. He watched helplessly as the men cut through the traffic with Spot and disappeared.

The door of the police station was open, and just inside we found the officer on duty bent over and writing at his desk. He looked up as we entered the room, but he went straight back to his work without saying a word. We were supposed to wait. He was alone except for a young prisoner who was standing behind him with his nose pressed against the wall, just like they used to make us do at school when we had misbehaved, our greasy little adolescent noses pressed against the blackboard while standing with our backs to the class in disgrace.

I told the nanny: "Tell the policeman why we are here. Tell him our dog has been stolen, we don't have time to waste," but she was too intimidated to interrupt him, and he continued to ignore us.

The prisoner, on the other hand, was curious to know why we were there and he kept turning around to ask the nanny more questions. Every time he turned to talk, the officer would shout at him to be quiet and to keep his nose against the wall. The police officer didn't speak English, so it was up to the nanny to explain why we were there. Once he realized we were talking about a dog, he made it clear that he wasn't going to waste valuable police time on a stolen pet. He more or less told us: "Bad luck," and then brushed us aside. We were supposed to have the good manners to leave so that he could finish what he was doing.

After the tension of the past few days, further exacerbated by my inability to speak Spanish and talk reason to the man, I suddenly exploded: "You might not think that our dog is important, but if someone in the building can hear me please help us!"

The policeman told the nanny to tell me to be quiet, but words that I had no power to control poured out of me. He watched in amazement as I transformed from a meek desperate woman into a tyrant. I told the nanny: "If he doesn't want me to talk then tell that idiot to arrest me!"

An idiot is similar to the same word in Spanish, so there was no need to translate. By then we were getting lots of attention. Heads were peeking out from adjoining rooms to see what all the commotion was about. The policeman was looking angry, and the nanny was petrified. She was afraid that we were both going to get arrested. She was now caught between her respect for and fear of the police, and her livelihood. He could no longer ignore us and began writing out a report while the nanny tried to smooth things over by grovelling and showing him the deference he expected. She reminded him that there would be a generous reward for him and his officers if the dog were recovered.

Tension poisoned the room, and I felt it might be more helpful for us if I tried to diffuse his anger by apologising and acting more respectfully. I told our nanny, "Please tell him that I want to apologise. I'm very sorry for my behaviour."

Even with his limited insight, he knew I didn't mean it. He glared back at me, which secretly pleased me no end. The only thing I was sorry about was that he hadn't understood half of what I said, and that I had no power to destroy him and ruin his career in the police force forever.

After our experience at the police station, I knew it was somehow up to me if I ever wanted to see Spot again. We caught a cab home, but I didn't have the heart to go in and face Nicky or my mother without Spot. Our situation seemed hopeless. The nanny and I walked up and down the street calling for Spot, hoping that by some miracle he had managed to elude his captors and that he was trying to find his way home. Then I remembered he didn't have Peruvian tags on his collar. He was still wearing his tags with our London address, and if the robbers couldn't find us to ransom Spot, he would never be coming home.

LOOKING FOR SPOT

I should have never left Nicky and my mother alone. She had no one to reassure her as she tried to comfort him. It hadn't occurred to me until later that she was grateful that only Spot had been taken. She held on to Nicky for dear life, and her fears of Peru multiplied out of control.

I kept my eyes on the ground as she pleaded, "Please come back to Florida with me. I don't want you to live here. It could have been Nicky. I want you to leave Peru. Isn't this enough to convince you that you are putting Nicky and yourself in danger? Does it take someone getting killed to bring you to your senses? I want you to come home."

Nicky was also begging, "Mummy I don't want to live here anymore. I'm afraid. I want to go with Grandma."

She told me, "This isn't a good place. You have to think of Nicky. He can't live like this. It's too dangerous. We're frightened. Nicky has just had Spot stolen, days after you were mugged. For God's sake, you've got to leave Peru!"

The problem was that she was leaving on Monday, which was three days away. I knew that if we left with her we would never see Spot again. Plus I had bought the apartment, and all of our furniture and belongings were in transit from London. I needed to be there when the shipment arrived, to sign papers and make other arrangements. There was also the problem of selling the flat. We were in too deep financially to just abandon Lima, but this didn't feel like an appropriate time to mention money. I rang Peter and he offered to catch the next plane back, but he had a business to run and at that point there wasn't anything we could do except wait. He was due to fly back in a few weeks, so we decided it was best if he kept with his plans and stayed in London.

I had no idea what to do or where to begin. I couldn't speak the language and knew next to nothing about how things worked in Peru. So I got on the phone and started asking everyone I had ever met for help. The first thing I needed was to give the thieves a way to contact us. Charo suggested posters, and she took me to have several hundred posters printed with a photo of Nicky holding Spot and our phone number. The posters also stated that there would be a generous reward for the dog, no questions asked. She arranged for a group of boys to put the posters up in the area where Spot was stolen.

Here was my excuse to move back to London. I had moved to South America and proven to myself that I could do it. Maybe now was the time to abandon ship and run. Nicky was begging me to leave Peru, as was my mother, but I had already bought the flat and until I was mugged and Spot was stolen we had loved living in Lima. That and all the terrifying possibilities surrounding Spot's fate; I couldn't just abandon him. However, until this problem could be resolved, we no longer felt safe living in Peru. After being mugged and having Spot stolen in the same week, Lima had become a frightening place.

My friends couldn't understand my reaction to the mugging. Giannina had warned me over and over again to be careful and never to walk down the street carrying a handbag, but I did. I felt invincible and took risks, so it didn't come as a surprise when they tried to rob me. I knew I was partially to blame. But after they robbed Spot and got so close to Nicky, I realized how vulnerable we were, and how irresponsible I had been.

My mother was mugged while we were living in London. It also happened at midday, in Chelsea, a few streets from where we lived. She was walking to a friend's house to play Bridge when a well-dressed man with a swarthy complexion approached her to ask the time. Mummy preferred small delicate watches, more feminine though difficult to read, and as she struggled to decipher the tiny numbers he grabbed the strap of her handbag; but she resisted and held on until the strap broke. After shouting a few choice expletives at the thief, she continued to the house to play Bridge. Her friends circled around her when she told them about the mugging. They listened in amazement and when she finished her story her friend Sheila took the broken handbag and handed her a stiff gin and tonic in its place. My mother never thought of leaving London after the mugging, nor had she become afraid; quite the contrary, we joked about it. She had cursed the thief, whom she called a "little bastard", which sent her friends into peals of laughter. They told me: "He certainly chose the wrong woman to rob. He will need counselling after tangling with your mother."

Every morning I got in the shower and cried until there were no tears left. I didn't want anyone to see my agony. In my mind, I saw Spot: hungry, terrified and alone. The day after Spot was taken an article appeared in the news, saying that the police had caught a gang of youths stealing defenceless dogs, to be thrown in with illegal fighting dogs and ripped apart as bait. I had no plan or direction. I was afraid that if I showed how lost and frightened I was it would make things worse for everyone. I had given up all hope, and then I remembered that we had a well-known celebrity with her own television show living above us. Gisela had been recognized in the lift by several of my friends. Young and beautiful, she was an energetic blonde with a popular TV talk show and was known for taking up causes and helping people. I had nothing to lose, so I wrote her a letter that was translated by a friend:

> Dear Gisela,
>
> I am so sorry to bother you and, under normal circumstances, I would never dream of imposing my problems on you, or invading your privacy and asking for a favour.
>
> But I am desperate and I don't know what else to do.
>
> We have just moved here from London and last night my five year old son Nicky had his dog Spot robbed out of his hands, on our street. Nicky is now terrified to live in Peru and wants to leave. Please help. We don't know where else to turn to but to you.
>
> I am enclosing a photo of Nicky and Spot. We would be very grateful if you could do anything to help us get Spot back.

None of my friends knew Gisela, so I asked my maid to ask Gisela's maid if she would take her a letter from me. Her maid already knew about Spot through one of the porters, and she was happy to take the letter; the news of our tragedy had spread quickly through the building.

That night Gisela helped us by telling our story on her program and by showing a poster of Nicky holding Spot with our phone number. Half of Lima watches her show and we were sure someone would recognize Spot and contact us. There wasn't anything we could have done on our own that would have reached so many people or gotten so much sympathy and attention, but there was still very little chance of getting Spot back, and if we didn't I had made up my mind to sell the flat and leave. My mother's last days in Lima were spent waiting next to the phone; hoping for news of Spot, praying he would be home before she left.

It was winter and the sky was shrouded in a damp blanket of grey. We were all depressed, and knowing my mother was leaving for Florida in a few days only added to our misery. It felt as if moving to Lima would end in total disaster. Within the space of a week, our happy carefree life there had changed forever. The phone never stopped ringing. People were saying, "We have your dog." But they weren't saying it in English and I couldn't talk to them. Between the television show and the hundreds of posters we put up around the neighbourhood, our phone number was everywhere. One of the first callers claiming to have Spot told us to meet them in a dangerous area of Lima, threatening: "Bring the reward money or else."

Our nanny answered the phone, and she was convinced that anyone who called had Spot. She cried and pleaded with me, "Please Señora Muffi, let me go with the money to meet them, we need to bring Spot home." I told her, "No. Tell them to prove they have Spot and then I will send the money. Everyone has seen his photo. They have to describe his tags, or that his baby teeth haven't fallen out and he has two sets of teeth. I won't meet them until I am sure they have Spot." With every call she begged, "Please, they have Spot. Señora Muffi, you don't know Peru, you don't understand. They might hurt him if you don't send money."

I felt torn in all directions. I didn't want to put Spot in danger by not following their demands, but it wasn't safe for us to meet them on our own. We didn't know if they had Spot or if it was just a trick to ambush us and get the money. We reached an impasse until Charo suggested we hire a bodyguard who was licensed to carry a gun. He would make the arrangements and negotiate the ransom with the thieves. The nanny would go with him to identify Spot; then they would pay the ransom and bring Spot home. In the meantime, he could protect Nicky.

The next day she brought over the former bodyguard of one of her friends. He was young and professional, ex-military or police.

Under armed protection, Nicky was allowed outside for the first time in days. Even so I insisted that they stay next to our building where I could watch, and where there were two policemen posted with guns to protect an ambassador who lived above us. Sometimes Nicky and I would go grocery shopping with the bodyguard, but aside from that we hardly went out. We needed to be close to the phone if someone genuine rang about Spot.

The following weekend the bodyguard took Charo and me to a market in the centre of Lima that was rumoured to sell stolen pets. He wanted to look for Spot, and pass around some of the posters showing a photo of Spot and our phone number. He also wanted to tell shop owners about the reward and explain we didn't want trouble; we wanted our dog back, no questions asked.

I looked conspicuously out of place and every once in a while, the bodyguard would adjust his jacket to show he was carrying a gun, warning potential muggers I wasn't a tourist who had strayed into the wrong place, and that I wouldn't be an easy prey. Nicky's face was on all the posters and after some of the excitement had died down we began to worry that with all the attention and publicity around Spot, someone might suppose if there was a huge reward for the dog, think what the child was worth! Nicky's photo had been shown on television, and there were posters of him and Spot on every street corner in San Isidro. He went everywhere with a bodyguard, which called attention to him. In Peru, it is better to keep a low profile. Kidnappings are less common nowadays, but they are still a threat. Everything I was doing to get Spot back was potentially putting Nicky in danger.

Armandina taught Nicky to recite a little story she invented: "I am a poor boy from Comas. My mother and I, we are very poor, we have no money for food. Even my grandmother has no money, she is very poor too. You see the colour of my hair? It is not real. It is dyed. I am just a poor little Peruvian boy from Comas." I told him: "Yes, that's right, poor is safe." Nicky wasn't shy about repeating what she had taught him, and I was asked by several maids in the building if I really dyed his hair, and, if so, which brand I used.

One man rang several times insisting he had Spot. He danced around the truth and told us, "I don't exactly have the dog in my possession. I am calling to negotiate the reward for my cousin and another boy who stole Spot and sold him to a neighbour. She has Spot, but I will collect him and bring him to you for the reward."

Later that day we got a call from a woman, who shouted into the receiver to be heard above the banging. She told us, "The boys that robbed Spot are trying to break down my door. They want him back for the reward." She told the nanny she had seen our story on television and she wanted Nicky to get his dog back. She said, "I don't want a reward; I only want the money I paid to buy him, and the money I spent when I took him to the veterinarian. I will bring you the receipts. When it is safe for me to leave the house, I will ring you."

We offered to send her our bodyguard, but she declined. She said she knew the boys. They were from her neighbourhood, and she didn't want to cause any more trouble. I didn't hold out much hope that we would hear from her again, but she had seen Spot. She read out the numbers and letters of our London address.

Then, a few hours later, she rang to tell us where to meet. We didn't know the area, or if we could trust her. I told the nanny: "She will have to meet us somewhere I think is safe. Tell her I will pay for her taxi to come to us." The woman agreed to meet near our flat where many of the cambistas - licensed moneychangers - do business in the street. They carry a great deal of cash, so we imagined that they would work in an area that was safe.

I didn't believe she would show up. We left the bodyguard with Nicky, and the nanny and I went to meet her alone. I brought four hundred dollars, just in case the woman changed her mind and we needed to negotiate a reward. It hardly seemed possible that this wasn't a trick; it seemed too easy. Yet, there she was with Spot on the opposite side of the road, exactly where we had agreed to meet. As we left the cab, I noticed a group of moneychangers huddled together holding one of our posters. They were looking across at Spot and the woman and then back at the poster, concentrating, comparing him to the dog in the photo trying to determine if it really was Spot. I panicked and dashed across the road, dodging traffic, afraid that at any second she might get frightened by their attention and run away. She smiled as I approached and stood up to hand Spot over to me. I thanked her, and then I buried my face in Spot's fur and cried, releasing all the pain and suffering I had carried with me for weeks.

The woman explained everything to the nanny. I couldn't understand most of what they were saying, but I watched as she produced the receipts from the veterinarian. Pugs have an odd way of breathing, with their snorts and grunts, but the family were not used to pugs and when they heard his noises they panicked and rushed him to the veterinarian, thinking he was gasping for breath. The person who wrote the bill copied the name off his tags: Spot de Bruyne, Carlyle Mansions, London SW3, so all the paperwork was in Spot's name with the London address. Other than getting a second set of vaccinations and losing weight, he looked fine.

I gave her a one-hundred dollar bill, far more than she had asked for, but it was a small way of showing my gratitude and also because I hadn't thought to bring change. We hugged goodbye, and as we thanked her she burst into tears and told us: "My daughter is heartbroken and stayed at home. She couldn't bear to lose Spot." The woman confided, "I bought Spot to replace her dog which had been stolen. Then I saw your story on television. My daughter is the same age as your son. That's why I returned Spot; I didn't want to be the cause of another child's suffering." When we crossed the street to catch a cab, all the money changers surrounded us and asked, "eSpot no?" They told us that they had seen Spot on television and in the posters. They said they had been watching her and were sure it was Spot, but they were too shy to approach the woman and ask, just in case it wasn't.

We told them: "Yes, it's Spot. He's going home."

All the moneychangers started cheering and clapping their hands. It felt as if all the goodness in the world had manifested around us. Money changing stopped momentarily while the cambistas, their clients, and people in the street, came over to ask questions and to touch Spot for luck. They were thrilled we had gotten him back and that they had been witness to his homecoming: "It's a miracle you found him again." Someone hailed us a cab and stuck one of our posters on the door. Even the taxi driver had seen Spot on television. Everyone waved us goodbye. We shouted back our thanks and the entire street cheered as we left for home.

Nicky was waiting by the door of the lift. He picked Spot up and ran into the kitchen to show Armandina. The first thing I did was to ring Peter and my mother to tell them the news. It was as if an enormous weight had been lifted from our lives. We had defied all the odds by bringing Spot home, but now there was the worry he could be robbed again. I bought a baseball bat and left it next to the service lift, and for weeks afterwards I was the only one allowed to walk Spot, which I did carrying the baseball bat slung over my shoulder, daring anyone to approach Spot and me.

After all the publicity everyone in Lima knew of Spot, and that we were willing to pay a handsome reward, no questions asked, if he was taken.

SPOT'S BIRTHDAY – 10TH AUGUST 2000

Spot's return was cause for celebration, and we invited a few friends over for lunch. Nicky wanted to invite Gisela, without whose help we wouldn't have had anything to celebrate. We had never met, but I knew she was busy with her show and she had her other businesses to run, so it hardly seemed likely she would come. I told Nicky, "Go ahead and invite her, write her a note and leave it with the Porter. She will be happy to hear from you even if she can't make it."

Armandina prepared Causa - yellow puréed potatoes layered with tuna, corn, tomato and avocado; and triple sandwiches made of avocado, egg, tomato and mayonnaise. She served salted quail eggs, deep fried cheese wrapped in wonton with guacamole, Papas a la Huancaina - boiled potatoes with a spicy cheese dip - and Yuquitas Rellenas – fried yucca root. For dessert Nicky baked a cake and decorated it by sticking a bag of chocolate kisses into the frosting. We ate too much and after everyone left we took a walk to digest.

When we returned the Porter told Nicky: "Señora Gisela came to see you, but when I told her you weren't home and she left." Nicky hadn't expected her to come so this was the worst possible scenario. He went upstairs to leave a message with her maid saying: "We are back, please tell Gisela to come see us when she gets home." I told him: "Nicky I'm sorry you missed her. Invite her another day." Nevertheless, it was a sad ending to Spot's fiesta.

Armandina had started clearing the table when the Porter buzzed us announcing: "Señora Gisela is on her way up." She came with her daughter, who had gone to the same school as Nicky, and she spoke English. And, as a greater surprise, they invited Nicky to join them in their country home for the weekend. Gisela also invited us to see them filming her television show the following week. A few days later, a friend of Gisela picked Nicky up and drove him to the country. I walked him to the car carrying his suitcase and a bottle of champagne for Gisela.

Nicky was in his element.

THE TELEVISION SHOW

When Nicky came home he talked non-stop. He told me: "Mummy, they had a barbecue at the house, and we swam. The water was freezing cold, but we jumped in anyway. There were lots of other children, and friends, and family of Gisela. I met Gisela's mother and her cousins. I let the guard dogs loose from their kennels and got in a little trouble. Don't worry, they didn't bite anyone and they were caught again."

It took him ages to calm down. When he finally did, he closed his eyes and slept for twelve hours straight. After he woke up, he started counting the days until he could watch them filming her show. He asked me: "Mummy, will you come with me to the show?"

Originally, I had planned to send him with Armandina. I wouldn't understand what they were saying, and I knew she would love to go, but since he had asked me to come with him I said yes. The show was on a school night and it started late, nevertheless it was educational and it wasn't an opportunity he would get every day. I didn't think it mattered if he stayed up and missed a day of school.

A young assistant of Gisela met us before the show and took us to the television studio. We had been asked to arrive early, long before the show was due to start. When we entered the studio, it was already packed with people. The next thing I knew, the girl who was in charge of us shuffled everyone around so we could sit in the front row. I wanted to stand at the side so Nicky could watch the filming and if he got restless we could slip away unnoticed. I hadn't realized there was an audience and that we would be part of it.

The show was in Spanish and I had never seen it before. We were told they finished filming at 11:00 p.m., which was much later than I had intended to stay. A couple in the front row were told to give up their seats for us. I tried to sit somewhere else. I knew they would have waited for hours to get seats in the front, but the person in charge told me to sit with Nicky and I couldn't speak Spanish well enough to insist that we sit somewhere else.

We were getting special treatment, so the people around us thought that we were important or connected with the show. One person asked if we were related to Gisela. All the people Nicky talked with had been in the audience before. They were devoted fans and regulars of the show. Nicky enjoyed the attention, but everyone was talking much too fast for me to follow, and I was bored to death.

The lights in the studio were intense and it was blazing hot. I was wearing all the wrong clothes, thinking that in winter a large studio would be freezing cold. People around us were dressed in tank tops, looking ready for the beach, while I wilted and withered in cashmere and a Marks and Spencer thermal vest.

Suddenly a man rushed out from the back, waving his arms, silencing us, and Gisela dashed into the room. The audience went wild. She came straight over to us and gave me a kiss. Kissing is the customary greeting between friends, but when she bent down to kiss Nicky he threw his arms around her neck, catching her off balance, and causing her to fall head first on top of him; it was an awkward moment and he didn't let go. We were being filmed and, without moving my lips, I pleaded with him: "Nicky! Let her go!"

Gisela is professional and kind, and you wouldn't have known from her face whether she had minded or not. Thank heavens that after her little struggle to recover her standing position she looked as beautiful and unruffled as when she first entered the studio. She continued greeting the rest of the guests as if nothing had happened.

That was the beginning, and things went from bad to worse. One of the cameramen said something to Nicky, teasing him about Gisela. But Nicky didn't like being teased, and he shouted something back at the man that I didn't understand. Nevertheless, I could tell by his reaction that what Nicky had said upset him. Now there was no way to escape. They were filming and we were trapped in the front row. Nicky and I had another talk. I told him: "Nicky, if you don't behave we're leaving," and he started crying.

He told me, "You are ruining everything. You don't understand Spanish. I didn't say anything bad to the man. I made a joke."

I told him, "That's not how it looked, he was upset."

He said, "I wish you hadn't come. I wish I had brought Armandina instead."

Funny how I was having the exact same wish. I worried it was going to look terrible for the show to see a child crying in the audience; and as I looked around I realized he was the only child there, which surprised me.

Next some young men and woman came out, modelling bathing suits. They stood posing, flaunting their taut, perfect figures, and holding large posters printed with questions, while other participants were brought in from back stage to answer them. One of the men wearing a bathing suit started dancing with Gisela. They were near the back of the studio, and the camera crew were blocking our view, which for Nicky was frustrating. We had to watch Gisela on the television screens installed on the upper corners of the room.

But Nicky had come to see her in person; after all he could watch her on television at home. So he jumped up and, before anyone could catch him, he ran over to Gisela. That caused a discernible gasp from the audience. Everyone knew Nicky was mine, and all eyes turned to me as if to say, "Gringa, get him under control."

I sunk further into my seat trying to look small and inconspicuous, but my head still towered above them and I stuck out like a sore thumb. One of the cameramen brought Nicky back to his seat and said something to me in rapid Spanish that I didn't understand.

Nevertheless, it was obvious he was annoyed. So Nicky and I had another talk with more tears. It was a school night, and he should have been at home, asleep or doing his homework. But there we were, captured on film, sitting in the front row of a popular reality show.

When the music stopped, Gisela began talking with a young girl seated next to her. Nicky filled me in saying, "Mummy she is one of the girls who lives in a house that Gisela has set up for the show." He told me, "Their lives are filmed and, when the audience gets bored with them, they are replaced; or they are automatically changed, I am not sure which."

This was all news to me, and my heart sank. I asked, "Oh my God, Nicky was this filmed where you spent the weekend?"

He said, "No Mummy, that isn't her real house, she doesn't stay there, it's only used for television."

I knew that sooner or later Peter would hear we were on the show and he'd say, "Have you lost your mind, appearing on a reality show with Nicky? He's in kindergarten for heavens sakes, it's inappropriate."

The girl talking with Gisela was adamantly denying something and she began crying. At first Gisela appeared to sympathize with her, but seconds later she instructed one of the technicians to put on a film taken by a camera in the House of Gisela, and we waited to see what would happen next.

Nicky and I looked up at one of the corner screens to see where everyone was looking, and we saw the girl Gisela was talking to covered by a thin sheet, apparently having sex with another person who was also part of the show. It must have proved beyond a reasonable doubt that the girl was telling less than the truth because she looked very surprised to see it, almost as surprised as I was. I thought, oh my God what next?

Nicky knew something was up and he asked me, "Mummy, what are they doing?"

Words failed me. I mumbled back, "I'm not sure," hoping to fob it off as some Peruvian custom I was not yet familiar with. Unsatisfied with my explanation, he began to question the people around us. They turned and looked daggers at me for the interruption, and for trying to pass the problem of his early sex education on to them.

After that, the theme changed and some of the performers came around the studio towards us. All the cameras were going, and the girl sitting next to us jumped up to dance with the man in the bathing suit. The people in the audience seemed to participate, or perhaps she was part of the entertainment. I was totally lost as to what was going on. Nicky took this as another opportunity to be with Gisela, who was standing there alone, watching. Again, a person working on the show brought him back to his seat. This time with a stronger warning directed at me. A bit later another woman was sent over to reiterate the message to keep him in his seat. At least I think that's what she said. I was going more by her body language and her hand motions, because I couldn't understand a word she was saying.

Under the circumstances, I wanted to leave. But, since we were sitting in a conspicuous place and we were Gisela's guests I was afraid it would look rude to leave in the middle of the show. Also there was the problem of what would happen if Nicky wouldn't come with me. It would disrupt the show even more if he had to be dragged out screaming. Children are great teachers of humility.

After a few hours there was an intermission, and I told Nicky that it was time to go home. By then he was behaving like an angel, and he walked over to Gisela who was in the back of the studio resting and kissed her goodbye while I waved goodbye from the exit. When we got home I poured myself a double Scotch and collapsed on the bed, trying to obliterate the last few hours from my memory, praying no one we knew had seen us on television. But that was impossible. In the morning the phone would be ringing off the hook.

I fixed myself another drink.

GETTING AROUND LIMA

I didn't buy a car in Lima. I have no sense of direction, nor do I have the nerve needed to drive alone in such a city. Getting around by taxi is easy. They're cheap, and there are hundreds of them. Anyone can put a taxi sign on their car and work, albeit not legally, but I have never heard of anyone getting into trouble. One of the problems is most of the drivers only know the main streets. They rarely carry a map, so it helps if you know where you're going, and can speak enough Spanish to direct them.

I was used to London where you could hand any cab driver the address and they knew the streets. You might be broke after paying their bill, but they knew where they were going and they respected the speed limit.

We were warned many times "never get into a Tico," which is a small inexpensive car often used as a taxi. Many people regard them as a death trap, but they are ubiquitous. There is a joke: "If you hit a pedestrian with a Tico he will survive, but everyone in the car will be killed or maimed." So we never used them, but we used other taxis that were just as risky. My mother loved telling the story that in one of the cabs I stopped the floor on her side of the car was missing. The hole was hidden under thick cardboard and mats, so she didn't notice until she stepped in and her foot went through to the road. We were in a hurry so I told her to keep her feet up. After that she always tested the floor before getting in.

Some of the younger taxi drivers in Lima drive so fast and so recklessly that I developed a renewed faith in God when I arrived in one piece. I used to fly aerobatics, but riding in a Peruvian taxi with no seatbelts, in the backseat, is a more death-defying experience. Sometimes I would renegotiate the price just to get them to slow down. At other times I would sit back while we whizzed in and out of traffic and enjoy the thrill.

Most of my friends in Lima drive the same way. They breeze through red lights; drive down one way streets in the wrong direction; stop anywhere convenient no matter how obstructive, illogical or dangerous; and turn around while driving to speak to you if you are sitting in the back seat.

Many of the taxi drivers had the gift of the gab, they loved to chat and give advice, going into great detail about which foods I should try, how to prepare them, and all the places I should see. There were endless suggestions on where to shop for bargains and who to vote for in the next election. One particularly animated taxi driver told me a story about a huge pileup on an autobahn in Germany. He swept the horizon with his hand saying: "There were cars everywhere, hundreds of cars involved in the accident. And while the police and rescue workers were going through the carnage searching for survivors, they found one car in the centre of it all that was untouched." Officials were in awe as they approached the driver, who by then was standing next to his car waiting for assistance, and they asked him: "How is it possible that out of all the cars here yours is the only one undamaged?"

He just shrugged his shoulders and told them: "No problem. I learned to drive in Peru. I'm used to keeping out of the way."

HAVE HAIR DONE

Once I had settled in and started adjusting to life in Lima, my friends showed me all the things I needed to know in order to venture out on my own and become more independent. One of the things I wanted to do was to get my hair cut, and a body perm. Giannina gave me the name and address of her hairdresser and told me: "I will make an appointment for you, and tell them what you want to have done. And as soon as I have time I will meet you there."

When I arrived at the hairdressers they were expecting me, but Giannina hadn't arrived yet. No one there spoke English. I wasn't sure what she had told them, or if they really knew what I wanted them to do. A woman took me over to the sink and started washing my hair, but there wasn't a word spoken between us, other than when I first arrived and we said hello.

While she was rinsing my hair the power to the street was cut. The lights suddenly flickered and failed, and the hairdryers went dead. The customers thought this was enormously funny, it created a common bond and they started chatting and laughing together.

No one seemed to mind that they could be stuck there for hours or that they might have to leave with wet hair. Everyone appeared to relish the situation. I thought of how different the customers' reactions would have been had it happened in London or New York, the panic and frustration, perhaps anger. I smiled back, unable to join in the fun. I couldn't wait to leave.

The lady doing my hair left the room and returned with an old rusty container, which she placed on the counter next to me. At first, I recoiled when she put it there, but then I relaxed thinking: "Don't be ridiculous, it can't possibly have anything to do with my hair." I distracted myself by imagining my friends in London watching me in this farcical situation at the hairdresser, unable to say a word to the person who was just about to cut and perm my hair. I began darting my eyes sideways at the rusty tin pretending that I was being filmed on location, documenting my epic adventure in Peru, which I would take back to London and use to entertain my friends. But all the while, deep inside, I was beginning to lose confidence, and praying to myself that the hairdressers only seemed primitive. After all, I knew Giannina wouldn't send me to a hairdresser who wasn't good. Still, I could see the humour in the situation. It was hard enough explaining something to my hairdresser in London, in English, when I wanted to try something new.

By the time she started putting the curlers in my hair, I was desperate. I wondered if it would be possible to run out of there without seeming hysterical or impolite. Thoughts whirled around my head: How much money should I leave her? Should I run? How will I catch a taxi on my own? How will I get home? I looked toward the front of the shop to plan my escape and lost heart after seeing the retractable security grille they had opened and then locked behind me as I entered. The woman doing my hair hadn't put the paper on the curler rods like hairdressers normally do. Nor were the curlers placed in any particular order. Some rollers fell to the floor and she laughed. Her technique filled me with dread, but there was no way of asking what she was doing. I continued praying that a miracle would happen and that help would arrive soon.

Then, to my horror, she started pouring the liquid from the rusty tin onto my hair. There was no way to tell her to stop. I couldn't remember the word! So I struggled to remove the various towels and waterproof coverings. Just as I stood up to run, the metal bars magically slid open and Giannina walked in. She looked at me and asked: "Gringa, what is the problem?"

I started firing off questions: "Have you ever seen a perm that she has done?"

"No," she said, "I told you I come here to have my hair cut."

I asked her, "Then how do you know if her perms are any good?"

She said, "I don't know if she is good. You asked me if I knew anyone who could make you a permanent and I said yes. Her husband is my hairdresser, but he doesn't do perms. He only cuts hair." Then for my absolute final unnerving, she told me, "The woman doing your hair isn't actually a hairdresser. She's my hairdresser's wife. She's just helping out and doing you a favour."

Since the chemical solution was processing my hair throughout the discussion I thought the damage had already been done. It was pointless to burst into tears and embarrass anyone. I let her finish her work. To my amazement, after it was washed and dried my hair looked natural. I had expected it to fall out in clumps, but in fact it looked great. Even so, I never had the nerve to go back again.

CHOCOLATE AT SCHOOL

A rmandina and I were decorating the Christmas tree when I got a call from Nicky's school. The teacher told me that Nicky had said he wasn't feeling well, so he was excused from playing football. She told him to remain on the side lines and watch the game, but when the children started playing he slipped away and took all the chocolate they had been given for Christmas and ate it. His teacher considered this to be the crime of the century, and premeditated. Plus, Nicky was so high from the chocolate that he hadn't shown any remorse whatsoever for what he had done. In fact, quite the contrary, he was in seventh heaven.

The teacher knew Nicky wasn't allowed sweets at home; it was something she couldn't understand. After all he was a child, and children eat sweets, as do most Peruvian adults. If I had allowed him to eat sweets as the other parents did he would not have been so desperate for the chocolate in the first place. That being the case I had contributed to the problem and was culpable. I rang Peter to keep him up to date with Nicky's latest mischief, and he wasn't amused. When I told him Nicky had taken the chocolate, he answered brusquely: "He did what?"

His response was harsher than I expected, so I tried to lighten the conversation by comparing "Nicky's crime" to some of the latest political scandals in Peru. I said, "It seems Nicky is showing real political promise."

He told me, "Get to the point. What are you talking about?"

I told him, "Nicky only needs a little more practice with misappropriation!"

Normally Peter hates my sense of humour, but he laughed saying, "Yes true, Nicky would be good in politics, a benevolent dictator. Don't worry, once he obtains power, he can hire someone to steal for him." But seconds later Peter sounded less jovial. He asked, "Nicky is not going to get thrown out of the school, is he? And I hope you didn't make a joke with his teacher. It's not funny."

After the chocolate incident, I compromised and let Nicky eat sweets. Peruvians are born with an innate desire for anything sweet and brightened up with a little food colouring. It was unfair for Nicky to live in Peru and to be brought up so differently from everyone else; we were already different enough.

It never ceased to amaze me how much things had changed from when I was in school. What was once thought of as naughty behaviour, and for which you either got smacked, humiliated in front of the class or sent to see the principal, is now considered a psychological defect. No more "boys will be boys." These days it's an automatic prescription for Ritalin. People want immediate results, and drugs have become the solution. Since there is now a quick chemical fix there is less incentive for teachers to take the time and work with disruptive children. I find it frightening how many children of Nicky's generation are medicated. It's hard to imagine there won't be repercussions from the children who have taken a cocktail of drugs all their lives instead of learning self-control. Peru is similar to the United States in that sense. They are pro psychiatrists and prescriptions for the latest drugs.

PARROT

Nicky and I talked about getting a parrot, and one night I saw Victoria, a girl who begged near our street, holding one. Her mother was chronically ill, so Victoria helped by begging after school. She waited at the traffic lights, and when the cars stopped she rushed over to sell the occupants sweets. I often saw her when I walked in the afternoon, and I gave her money and clothes which Nicky had outgrown, so she knew me. She would run over with her grandmother to kiss me when I walked in the afternoon, but they hardly understood me when I spoke.

When I saw Victoria with the parrot, I begged my date to stop and ask where I could buy a tame one like hers for Nicky. That's when she told him that this parrot was for sale. Before I could say no, he bought it for me. It was late, and I wasn't expecting a parrot, but I knew Victoria needed the money so I accepted the unwilling bird and put it inside my coat as she instructed.

The bird quickly settled down, resigned to his fate. When we arrived at my building there was no problem smuggling him past the Porter and into the lift, but just as we pushed the button to go up the Porter opened the door, stopping the lift and allowing another couple to enter. Neither of them noticed Charlie. His head was barely visible, peeking out beneath my chin however when the lift moved he let out a shriek that left little doubt about his presence. I apologized, but they hadn't heard, they were all deaf. When the lift stopped we shot out, hoping they wouldn't report Charlie. I left him in the kitchen, in a basket with the vegetables, and made us a drink.

In the morning Charlie was a vague memory, until I entered the kitchen and saw Armandina's face. She didn't expect an explanation as to why there was a parrot in the kitchen pooping on her vegetables and causing pandemonium, but I could tell that she would have been happier if he had been left in the jungle where he belonged. Charlie on the other hand was delighted to see me, and once he caught hold of me with his sharp little claws he wouldn't let go. There was no way to disentangle myself without a struggle and more deafening screeches, so I took him to my room and started typing my book. He in turn started pooping down my back and cooing in my ear, while entertaining himself by removing my bright orange earplugs. In the light of day Charlie was a huge mistake, but Nicky had already seen him, and Charlie was absolutely irresistible when he did his soft little coos and rubbed his face up and down my neck. He trusted me enough to allow me to put my fingers through his dense wiry feathers and stroke his warm delicate flesh.

My Spanish teacher cringed when she heard Charlie in the kitchen. She couldn't understand why I had brought him home. She thought parrots were loud, filthy and obnoxious. As she told me, "Good words to remember." But even so she knew where we could buy a birdcage, so we caught a cab and continued my Spanish lesson en route. The cab dropped us at the entrance of a busy market that opened before dawn, but the shop that sold cages was still padlocked shut. While my teacher was asking one of the vendors when the shop opened, or if they knew somewhere else nearby where we could buy a cage, I saw a man wandering around naked. He was in his early twenties, maybe thirties; it was impossible to tell his age. His hair was matted and filthy, and he looked as if he had never bathed. He kept his eyes to the ground, as if searching for something. Perhaps he was looking for food or anything else that might come in useful. I watched him through the corner of my eye and remembered Poor Tom, who as a student I had seen in King Lear, walking stark naked across a London stage. Poor Tom was also covered in dirt and twigs. Poor Tom was only feigning insanity, but he was the only other man I have seen wandering around dirty and naked, and it made a lasting impression.

The other people in the market didn't appear concerned by the naked presence. He wandered through them as though invisible. They flowed around him, keeping a small but imperceptible distance away. For me it was very disconcerting having him around, and I found my eyes following him, not understanding how anyone could be so at ease having a naked madman walking freely among them. My Spanish teacher saw me watching and explained, "There are few options for him. His family must work and they can't keep him locked in the house all day. He isn't bothering anyone, so people leave him in peace. There but for the grace of God go all of us."

One day I heard laughter coming from the kitchen, and I listened as Nicky explained to Armandina and Irma that he was studying Darwin at school. He told them that we had evolved from apes, and that according to Darwin it was evolution, not God, that was directly responsible for their creation. I wanted to clarify Darwin's theory as best as I could with my limited Spanish, and as I entered the kitchen I saw Charlie glide down and start running in Spot's direction. At first Spot stood his ground. He hated Charlie, who had taken over both his kitchen and our attention. However, Spot quickly changed his mind and tried to run, but unable to gain traction on the tiled floor he couldn't move. Charlie bit hold of Spot's tail, and Spot sprang forward, jerking Charlie into the air like a kite. Charlie was hanging onto Spot's tail, wildly flapping his wings to keep upright. He wasn't bored now. Spot collapsed in a heap, and I grabbed Charlie before he did any more damage to Spot's self-esteem.

A few days later I went into the kitchen to cover Charlie's cage, and he was gone. Nicky and I searched the neighbourhood for days, but we never found him. I know he was encouraged to leave; the window was left open. Escaped parrots were so numerous in our neighbourhood that when the local flock swooped or turned in unison, the sky flashed green for a second. I was happy Charlie was free.

But I hoped we might see him again.

THE SPANISH TEACHER AND
THE FLOOD

I got an unusually early phone call from a stranger, saying he had a message for me from my Spanish teacher, who was late. He explained that he was the foreigner living with her sister and they were the only ones in her family with a phone. Veronica had called him from her roof, to say they had survived the flood, and asked him to pass the message on to her family, and then to call me because I was waiting.

I have heard many excuses for employees not showing up to work, but this one was so absurd that I became curious and I asked Armandina to switch on the local news. There it was! The river had overflowed and people were stranded on their roofs. Reporters had gone out in boats to film for the local news, but no one had come out to help them. I tried to ring Veronica, but her cellular phone was dead.

When Veronica returned to teaching the following week, she described how water flooding into their bedroom had woken them up, and she had escaped onto the roof in the dark with her husband and baby son. They were grateful be alive and not to have drowned like one of the neighbours. But they lost everything. Most of what they owned was bought on credit, and they weren't insured, so they would have to start again, but burdened with a larger debt. Her husband returned to work, but he was sent home and told not to come back until he could find his uniform or replace it. She said that although the local government would send aid, the people who needed it most were the least likely to get it.

Veronica continued teaching, but she wasn't feeling well. We imagined it was from stress. Their adobe house had absorbed so much water it would never be habitable again. Having no other choice, they moved in with her in-laws, where they had no privacy and little space. After feeling ill for weeks she went to the doctor, and found out she was pregnant. I watched her quiet resolve. They had no home, no possessions, plus there would be one more mouth to feed; and she couldn't teach and take care of a newborn baby. All their future plans had suddenly changed.

When I told Nicky about the flood he asked, "Did God send the flood to punish them for being bad?" He was preparing for his First Communion and we had been talking about Noah's Ark. So it was a reasonable question.

I told him, "No good people also have bad things happen to them."

He asked, "Why?"

I said, "I don't know. God didn't send a flood to punish them. They lived next to a river and rivers flood. It's nature. The developers were greedy; they shouldn't have built houses so close to a river without putting in a seawall or some other form of protection. That tragedy was manmade, but they will probably get away with it because the victims can't afford lawyers to represent them. Without lawyers, it is difficult to find justice. God doesn't need to send floods any more people are punishing each other."

"Then what's the point of being good?" he asked.

SCHOOL FLOODED

I hated getting phone calls from Nicky's school, and I could tell by the tone of voice that this call was bad news. English was not the teacher's first language, and she kept lapsing into Spanish to better express some deep grievance that involved Nicky. After she had calmed down and I could better understand her, I realised what he had done. "Nicky has flooded the school. He went into one of the bathrooms and blocked up all the sinks and showers with earth. Then he turned the water on full volume and left."

I feigned disbelief saying, "There must be a mistake. Why do you think it was Nicky? Are there witnesses?" My voice lacked conviction, but I couldn't imagine why he would have done such a thing.

The staff had been searching for the perpetrators of the crime, forming a dragnet across the school. Teachers were questioning teenagers, thinking they were the most likely culprits, not a six year old. Then one of the maintenance men came forward and mentioned that he had seen Nicky in the area; and when a teacher confronted Nicky, he didn't hesitate to admit he had done it.

Nicky always told the truth, which was extraordinary at his age. It often got him into trouble, but you can count on him for telling the truth. Sometimes I felt like suggesting to him that when he had done something really insane, like flooding the school, why not be a tiny bit naughtier and lie about it. When Nicky arrived home I asked, "Nicky what is going on? A teacher told me you flooded the school."

Then, suddenly, it all made sense. Both of the women working for us had taken the same day off, an exception to the rules. Nicky felt it was unjust that they had abandoned him, leaving me alone to cook, so he devised the flood. Like Jesus who suffered for our sins, Nicky felt all workers should suffer because of our cook! So much for religious classes and youthful interpretation.

As punishment, Nicky was banned from playing football until further notice. What they didn't know was that Nicky hated football. He hated all regimented sports, except swimming, and it was sheer joy for him to be banned from playing. After that I prayed he didn't make a regular feature out of flooding the school, or doing something worse, now that he had discovered how easy it was for him to get out of sports.

THIRD PERUVIAN ELECTION
3RD JUNE 2001

After an interim period, the campaign posters went back up and Peru prepared for another round of elections. Delegates from the Organization of American States returned to ensure that this time everything was done according to the rules. Most of the candidates from the first round were running, including Alejandro Toledo.

Out of the blue, ex-president Alan Garcia arrived in Bogotá and announced that he was returning to Peru to run again for president. Garcia's first tenure as President, from 1985 to 1990, was marked by terrorism, corruption, food shortages, and hyper-inflation, which peaked at more than 7,000 per cent. In economic terms, his government was one of the worst in Peruvian history. However, he had taken on an economy that was already in shambles from the outgoing president, and at the time he was elected Garcia was thirty-six years old. He lacked experience and the expertise to resolve such complex financial issues. Or maybe, as some believed he was corrupt. He waited outside the country until The Supreme Court of Peru ruled that corruption charges against him from his previous term of office had expired and that he could return and not be arrested.

When Garcia's tenure in office had ended he didn't run for a second term because he didn't have a chance of winning. Perhaps he thought he could maintain power through his strength in Congress. But he underestimated President Fujimori's strength, and when he overstepped his position, Fujimori sent soldiers to arrest him. Garcia escaped over the rooftops, and for eight years he and his family lived in exile in Paris. Many people who had lived through his presidency were not enthusiastic to see him back. His critics claimed he bankrupted the country through his ambition and incompetence. He attempted to nationalize the banks and the insurance industry, and further angered the financial community by unilaterally drawing up a limit to debt repayment equal to 10 percent of the GNP, which cut the country off from international investors. Garcia had been a disaster as President, but now there was a new generation of voters who were too young to remember his era, and they were looking for a dynamic leader like him.

My friends were divided on the subject. A few confessed they might vote for him given the other choices, and because they were confident he would make amends to rid himself of the stigma of being the worst President in Peruvian history. Others were saying, "Once a thief always a thief!"

Within weeks of campaigning, Garcia had shot up in the ratings, but after a close race Toledo was elected president. He fought well against the opposition and helped force the resignation of President Fujimori. The press were having a field day with their reinstated freedom; spewing tales of his drinking and womanising, and that he had tested positive for cocaine. He also refused to take a DNA test to prove conclusively that a young girl who was claiming to be his daughter wasn't.

Toledo met his wife Eliane while they were students at Stanford University, and they married in 1972. She was foreign, born in Paris to a Polish father and a Belgian mother. After earning a BA in anthropology in Jerusalem, she had gone to the United States to study anthropology. After graduation, Toledo worked at the UN and then at the World Bank as an economic advisor. Later they moved to Peru where he worked for the Ministry of Labour. He went on to teach economics, while his wife researched indigenous communities and became fluent in Quechua. In 1990, Toledo returned to the United States and took a research job at Harvard. During that time, they separated and she returned to Israel. In 1994, Toledo went back to Peru and started "País Posible" and ran against the popular incumbent Alberto Fujimori. Toledo lost, but he finished with a respectable percentage of the vote. In 1995 Toledo reunited with Eliane and started his second campaign for president.

Nicky and I moved to Lima in 2000, when Toledo ran against Fujimori again. This time he went from being a little known candidate to leader of the opposition against Fujimori's presidency. By then Peru had fallen into recession and people wanted change. Toledo campaigned as "El Cholo" – "The Indian", running to become Peru's first indigenous president, which gave him an advantage with much of the population. His wife proved to be an asset during the campaign. She wooed the audience by dressing in native Andean dress and by giving speeches for him in Quechua, an indigenous language spoken by close to ten million Peruvians that allowed her to connect directly with a large group of voters many of the other politicians couldn't reach.

During her work in indigenous communities Eliane became familiar with the traditions and superstitions of Peru, which she used to her husband's advantage. At one rally, she roused the crowds by claiming the mountain God Apus had spoken, saying Toledo would be elected President. This would make him Peru's first democratically elected President of Indian descent, thus ending hundreds of years of oppression. Eliane ingratiated herself with the poor and forgotten voters, some of who felt that she too was sent by the gods to help them, but her love for underprivileged Peruvians didn't extend to the oligarchy. They reciprocated her dislike by describing her as an intelligent but brash, unkempt egoist with an enormous chip on her shoulder.

MOM ARRIVES AGAIN

B y my mother's third trip to Lima we were independent. I knew my way around, and my Spanish had improved. It was a mild winter and we were often out doing things on our own. Lima is twelve degrees south of the equator, and normally it should have a tropical climate, but because of the Humboldt Current, which flows up from Chile and brings arctic water with it, high humidity is formed as it hits the warm air along the coast. The mountains to the east then block the heat and rain from reaching the coast, making it sub-tropical. Lima is one of the driest capital cities in the world. It hardly rains, but during the winter humidity runs at over 90 percent, saturating the air with visible moisture, causing everything to feel damp and disagreeable. July isn't the ideal month for a visit, but my mother preferred the climate of Lima to the unrelenting heat in Florida.

One of our favourite places to go was the Artisan Market in Miraflores, where I discovered a showcase packed full of reproduction huacos eróticos - pornographic huacos. Huacos are pottery figures that were buried with the dead. They are a physical record, depicting hunting, agriculture, war, human sacrifice, torture, sex, and disease. Some of the original huacos are dated to more than fifteen hundred years ago. There are many different types sold, but the ones that captured my attention were the erotica.

Huacos eróticos, also called pornograficos, were once hidden away from the public, sealed away in the repositories of museums and only accessible to small groups of scientists. The sexually explicit figures included sodomy, homosexuality, cunnilingus, bestiality, necrophilia and blowjobs. Nowadays they have celebrity status, and are prominently displayed in museums.

The huacos I found were good reproductions; the seller claimed that his were made from original moulds, taken from tombs. The copulating figures were hard to pass by without taking a closer look. Their brazen sexuality attracted many surreptitious smiles and whispers, but no takers. I hesitated to ask the price with other customers present, and wandered up and down the counter rubbing alpaca shawls between my fingers, pretending to be interested in other things, and kept up the masquerade until the other customers had left. Then I hastily negotiated a price for five or six figures; it was quicker to buy them in bulk and decide which I liked best at home.

Alfred Kinsey, a pioneer in human sexuality, came to Peru in the 1950s to examine the huacos eróticos and called them, "the most frank and detailed document of sexual customs ever left behind by an ancient people." Many of the huacos were smashed in the 1500s by the church, whose priests were sent from Spain to reform and convert the natives to Christianity. To the church the huacos represented sin and depravity, and they were immoral to a Spanish clergy intent on eradicating idolatry, masturbation, homosexuality, trial marriages, sodomy, and all forms of art depicting sexual pleasure. At the time, the indigenous population placed no particular importance on female chastity, except for those few needed for sacrifices. It took torture and harsh punishment to convert a natural, joyous race to the Christian mores of sex being only for procreation and to convince women they were not supposed to experience sexual pleasure.

My mother offered to take a few huacos back and leave them in a friend's shop, in order to test the market in Sarasota. I would have been mortified to take them through customs. I couldn't imagine being pulled aside and asked to unwrap a figure of a man having sex with an alligator, or one of the other bizarre things they were up to, but Mom wasn't concerned in the slightest. She was having a wonderful trip - until we spent the day in the mountains of Los Condores, with Chan, basking in the sun. When we returned to the cold damp of Lima, the change of climate was too much, and by the next morning she felt too ill to get up. After spending several days in bed, I sent for the doctor, but he couldn't cure a cold. After that all Mom talked about was home.

Giannina rang and told me: "Quick, run, turn on the news! A plane has hit one of the twin Trade Towers." I switched on the news and saw a black spot on the side of one of the towers. The newscaster was saying an airplane hit it, which seemed impossible. The camera was filming the tower, and then, in the distance, I saw another plane turning in. I thought it had gone off course to see what had happened to the first plane until it exploded against the second tower. At first, I waited for an explanation. I wanted to make sure it wasn't science fiction or a graphic simulation of a terrorist attack before I woke my mother.

We watched the news together; it was replaying footage of the second airplane hitting the building over and over again. Then there was an enormous explosion, a dense cloud of dust, and both buildings were gone. My mother was lying next to me in bed, wrapped in blankets. The cold and damp were inescapable, seeping in through every window, saturating the air with a relative humidity of close to 100 per cent. During winter Lima is often described as "living in an aquarium", the air is so saturated it feels like breathing in liquid. The climate is mild but disagreeable; mould thrives, metal blisters and rusts, arthritis and rheumatism flare up, and lungs congest. Every winter someone laments, "It was the Incas who tricked Pizarro, the Spaniard who conquered their Empire, into making Lima the capital city of Peru. Knowing the dampness would make the Spaniards ill, and that they and their families would suffer in perpetuity."

My closet resembled a laboratory experiment. Even the fifteen heating bars lining the walls couldn't control the humidity. The moist, comforting warmth within the closet brought a variety of unseen spores to life. Racks of shoes and handbags germinated and sprouted a myriad of colourful fungi, looking like Petri dishes lined up in rows. My bed felt damp to the touch, and my mother claimed that she could only endure her last few days in Lima because she knew she was leaving soon.

The two of us remained in front of the television for the rest of the day, hardly speaking, wondering what would happen next. We lived in London during the IRA bombings and witnessed the grisly aftereffects, but neither of us had ever contemplated terrorism on this scale, especially not in the United States. The news demonstrated our vulnerability and brought home the terrorists' callous disregard for life. I was also in a panic, because my mother was booked to fly back to Florida in three days. Even after seeing the news of three planes down, and listening to recorded messages from passengers saying their last goodbyes to family and friends, she was determined to leave.

My mother knew what I was thinking and warned me, "Muffi I'm leaving, this is not open for discussion." I begged her to change her mind and to stay longer, at least until they had better security in place, but after being sick all she wanted was to go home. Fortunately, all flights were cancelled to and from the United States.

It was hard to imagine how much our circumstances had changed from her last visit to Peru. This time Nicky and I were begging her to stay in Lima, pleading with her not to go back to Florida.

With terrorism, anthrax in the post, and the fear of more reprisals in the United States, suddenly Peru felt like the safest place.

GIANNINA MUGGED

P eter and I were invited to a dinner party which was miles away;
so, we arranged with Quique and Giannina to meet at my flat
in order to drive there together. When the doorbell rang I knew it
was Giannina; she was always on time or early, which was rare in
Peru, so without asking who it was I pushed the buzzer to let her in.
The instant I pushed the buzzer I heard a bloodcurdling scream
from below. When no one responded over the intercom I ran to
the window overlooking the front door, and watched as someone
struggled to get up from the steps. The person appeared inebri-
ated, stumbling as they climbed towards the entrance. I thought,
"Damn. Where is the Porter? He had better get rid of this person
quickly before my friends arrive."

Then my eye caught the motion of someone crouching in a
shadow near the street, and suddenly a car screeched over to him.
The man, lithe and graceful as a gymnast, leapt from the shadow,
flung himself in through the open window, and the vehicle sped
away. I watched as the car disappeared down the street. The doorbell rang again, but this time I let Armandina answer. Seconds later I heard a scuffle and Giannina screaming in the hallway. When

Armandina opened the door of the lift Giannina staggered out, almost falling into the room.

Peter and I did our best to calm her as she told us, "As I turned my back to the street to ring your doorbell, a man came up behind me, grabbing the strap of my handbag, choking me and pulling me backward down the steps. He has my handbag."

I had a drink while Giannina and Peter got on the phone to cancel her credit cards. There was no mention of reporting the robbery to the police.

Quique was the last to arrive. He made a habit of being late. He was one of the first people I met in Lima, and we instantly became friends. We both lived in London during the early seventies, a few streets away, and had friends in common, but it wasn't until Salvador introduced us at a party in Lima that we met. I already knew who Quique was, he was famous in my circle of friends in the seventies; he was young, charming, and single; a gentleman playboy who drove exotic sports cars, loved to dance, entertained lavishly, and partied all night. I was also thrilled when I met him because I knew he spoke English.

But Quique hadn't practised his English for years. He was more at ease speaking Spanish and he persisted: "Don't you know any Spanish?"

I said, "No." I wanted to talk to him about London. I wanted to talk about anything in English.

He asked, "Surely you know some Spanish, you must have learned something?"

I told him: "Quique, I have lived in Lima for a couple of weeks. You lived in London for years. You learned English at school when you were young. I haven't learned Spanish yet." He wouldn't relent. After a few drinks, I told him: "Yes, I know a few words of Spanish: "Quiero cachar!" - which roughly translated means, "I want to fuck!" He was shocked when I said it, and then I innocently asked him, "Doesn't that mean I am pleased to meet you?"

He told me: "No, no, it doesn't."

I said, "No?" And playing with some strands of hair, twirling them around my finger, I asked, "Oh dear. What does it mean? Teach me." However, he preferred not to explain the meaning and has never spoken to me in Spanish since.

There was nothing we could do to help Giannina, so I fixed us a drink and we talked while they tried to get through and cancel all Giannina's credit cards. When everything was sorted out she said, "Let's go to dinner," which surprised us. She was bruised and dishevelled, but she was concerned that four people missing from the table would spoil the dinner and that it wasn't fair to our host.

I was disappointed to hear we were going. Unbeknownst to anyone there I had received a phone call from a friend informing me that our host, the man I had been dating for several weeks, came to her building every Saturday morning to spend the day with his secretary. She seemed surprised I didn't know. I had been grateful we were going to miss the dinner and that I wouldn't have to be there, pretending to enjoy his company. But Giannina wanted to go, and I didn't want to burden her with my problems or be dramatic and ruin the evening for everyone.

When we went down in the lift, Quique asked the Porter why no one had gone out and helped Giannina. The front of our building was glass. The Porter and his two companions saw the mugging. They were standing a few feet away, but they hadn't helped her. The Porter told him: "The robber only wanted her handbag. She should have let go. She can replace a handbag. We have families. If one of us had gone out we might have been killed or maimed for interfering, who would have looked after our families?"

IGUANA

When Peter was in Lima, he made a point of meeting with Nicky's teachers, because when I was on my own I tended to shy away from the school. Peter was charming with them, whereas I struggled with the language and was defensive with the constant criticism over Nicky's behaviour. The school was miles away. To get there we took the highway which cuts through Lima. Vendors surrounded the car at every traffic light, selling soft drinks, newspapers, toys, pirated DVDs and books. I always looked at what they were selling, and if I saw something I wanted to buy I asked our driver to bargain for me.

While we were stopped at a light I watched a man holding an iguana above his head. He saw that I was interested, and ran over to give me a closer look. I wanted to buy it for Nicky. I just needed the driver to negotiate the price. But Peter was in the front talking with him, and by the time I got their attention the light changed, forcing us to move with the traffic or cause pandemonium. I was miserable. I wanted Nicky to have all the exotic pets I had been forbidden to keep when I was young. We searched for the seller on the way home, but we never saw him again.

Peter was relieved that I hadn't bought the iguana. He would have hated having it in the car with us. He isn't enamoured with reptiles and could never understand why I would want to buy such a creature for a pet. He reminded me: "Nicky still bares the scar on his face from one of the turtles you bought him. Why would you risk bringing home an iguana? Didn't you see its claws?"

I told him: "Peter stop, don't go on about the turtles. They were the prizes for his grades. I didn't want them; terrapins are usually covered with salmonella. I had said no. But the sales girl intervened. They were both begging. It was awkward. She swore they were healthy and wouldn't bite. But in all fairness, I'm sure when she was selling them to me she hadn't expected Nicky to kiss one good night."

Months later, I saw another man selling an iguana, but this time the driver saw him too and he stopped to buy it for me. I had never held an iguana before, and seeing it up close with its dull spiky armour and sharp claws was more frightening than I had expected. My driver rolled down his window to negotiate the price, but after the money changed hands he ducked as the vendor handed the iguana through his window directly to me. The driver wasn't happy having it on the seat behind him. He knew from my hesitancy to take it that I was frightened, and that if the iguana bit me or wriggled to escape, my instinct would be to get it as far away from me as possible. That being the case it would almost certainly be thrown forward in his direction.

Nicky was initially thrilled with the iguana and named him Paco, but he quickly lost interest, and I took over feeding Paco and keeping him company. It didn't seem fair that he was caged, but I couldn't let him run loose in the apartment, and I couldn't set him free; he might starve, or a dog would get him. The weather was cold and damp and we had no central heating, so Paco had no way of keeping warm other than sitting on my lap or on my shoulder. When I held him, his sharp little claws dug into my skin, which hurt. I found out that iguanas aren't the easiest animals to develop affection for. Sometimes I heard him scratching to escape, which made me feel guilty. The sound of his misery caused me to stop what I was doing and pick him up.

One morning Nicky came bursting through my bedroom door in tears. I sat up dazed. My eyes had barely opened when he dropped Paco in my hand and asked: "Mummy is he dead? Is he dead? Please, Mummy, take him to the doctor. Tell him to make him well. Please, Mummy, help him, do something!"

After having a cold dead animal thrust into my warm sleepy hand, I thought I was going to be sick, especially as I was already feeling frail from a dinner the night before. All I really wanted to do was to scream, jump out of bed, and fling the cold lifeless body across the room just to get it out of my hand. Then afterwards shake my hands violently to lose the sensation.

I've always hated touching dead animals, and this one was in bed with me. I managed to calm Nicky down and found a shoebox with some tissue paper. We gently wrapped Paco and said a prayer as we laid him in the box. Nicky went to the park with Armandina to bury him, and by lunchtime Paco was no longer a tragedy; not forgotten, but the tears had ended.

My first pet was a goldfish and when it died I was inconsolable for weeks. Goldie was only partly mine. I shared her with my grandfather, who sent her over with his other fish when he closed his house in Florida to escape the summer. One day she floated to the surface of the pond, gasping for breath, and when she died I sat by her body all day and wept. I was relieved that Nicky wasn't devastated over Paco's death. Grandpa and I were sentimental to a fault as far as pets were concerned. He would stay in bed for days when one of his dogs died, and cried out in agony when he found a stork standing in the middle of his pond spearing and then swallowing the last of our goldfish. Joseph, who worked for grandpa, never forgave himself for scrubbing the pond clean of Anacharis plants and algae, thereby leaving no hiding place for the fish. Their plump, glistening bodies attracted the hungry birds, and the moment Joseph left to find grandpa so he could show him the pristine pond, the birds descended. Grandpa never had the heart to replace them, and it was years before I got another pet.

LUNCH AT NASCA

Nasca is famous for its "Lines" and figures drawn across the surface of the desert. The Nasca Lines are believed to pre-date the Incas, and were first mentioned in 1547 in Cieza de León's Chronicles. There are many theories as to why they were created, ranging from landing strips for extra-terrestrials, to an ancient calendar created by the Nasca civilization. One theory is that the lines were never intended for human eyes, because they are best understood from above. Another theory is that they were made after a total solar eclipse of the sun, known then as the Eye of God, when the dark sphere of the moon blocked the sun and its light spilled out around the edges causing it to look like a fiery iris peering down at them from heaven. Another theory is that the King of Nasca worried about the expanding population and how he could provide enough food to keep his subjects fed. He ordered the Lines built as a form of birth control, because after working on them all day his subjects were too exhausted for sex.

The most recent theory is that the lines were used as extra-terrestrial landing strips. Some of the lines stretch for miles and are visible on satellite photos. The Nasca Lines were first spotted from the air in the 1920s, when commercial flights began crossing the desert. Pilots and passengers reported seeing what they thought were landing strips and images on the ground below. Paul Kosok, an American professor from Long Island University, came to Peru in the 1930s to do a field study on the relation of irrigation to settlement patterns of ancient cultures. When his tenure was over he asked Maria Reiche, his assistant, to continue the work, and she remained in Nasca and dedicated the rest of her life to understanding their meaning. Reiche was known to disappear for weeks at a time into the dessert with a broom, to sweep away the small pebbles and debris that the wind had deposited in the shallow furrows of the lines. She said, "To make them more accessible for viewing I cleaned them with a broom, one broom after another throughout the years. I went through so many brooms that rumours circulated that I might be a witch."

Her work in Nasca attracted worldwide attention; and she used her influence and the profits from her books to campaign for their preservation. Until then their importance hadn't been widely recognized and people were permitted to farm and drive across the drawings, which has left permanent damage. There is also a main highway cutting across part of one of the figures, and commercial mining a few feet away. The total area of the Nasca Lines covers approximately 450 square kilometres.

While Nicky and I waited for a plane to take us up we were shown a brief film about the history of Nasca. At first, I wasn't paying much attention to the film. It was in Spanish, and difficult for me to understand, but I watched, and the narrator caught my attention by holding up an enormous and unusually shaped skull. He explained: "The unusual size and elongation of the skulls were not from cranial binding. Cranial deformation changes the shape, but not the volume of the head." These craniums were almost double the normal size, and where the spinal cord passes through is in a different place; irrefutable proof, according to the filmmaker, that some of the early people of Nasca had bred with spacemen. I believe that's what he said, but maybe part of it was lost in translation.

Quique's family once owned vast cotton estates in Nasca, but in the early 1970s they were expropriated under General Juan Velasco and the family were given Bonds in its place. The Reforma Agraria - Land Reform Act - was introduced to diversify the ownership of farmland, and break up the holdings of idle absentee landlords, improving production by redistributing the land to the workers. Quique's land had produced two million five-hundred-thousand quintals of cotton a year when the family owned and managed it, but during the land reform under President Velasco the government redistributed the land to labourers who had no idea how to run a commercial business. Nor were they given the equipment needed to farm it commercially, as the government offered no technical training or financial assistance. Nowadays, the property is so divided that commercial farming is no longer viable.

The house was returned to the family with a few acres, but without the income from the cotton to maintain it, so they turned it into a hotel to help cover expenses. Some of the labourers who were given the land were also left without an income, so they came to Quique for help and earned a meagre living by working for him at the hotel. During the land reform, President Velasco took Peru back to the Stone Age agriculturally. The country became dependent on importing sugar and potatoes, which originated in Peru. Up until the Reforma Agraria these foods had been grown in abundance. Vast estates were destroyed during Velasco's reign, and to this day only a few have recovered their original productive capacity.

Quique's family had organized a lunch for Lourdes Flores, a hugely popular politician who had been the Conservative candidate in the last presidential elections. Although she hadn't won many people felt it was only a matter of time before she became President. She was strong in government, and they wanted to keep her up to date with the problems affecting tourism in Nasca, which included the problem of no direct flights from Lima, which affected accessibility to one of the world's great wonders. Flores was due to arrive late morning, and before dawn preparations began in honour of her visit. Long tables were hauled out of storage, wiped down, and arranged across the lawn for the buffet. One of the employees dug a hole near one of the tables for the pachamanca; Nicky watched them slit the throat of their lunch, outside our room. A pachamanca is prepared by lining a hole in the ground with bricks forming an oven, then rocks are heated and shovelled in, next layers of potatoes, corn, and a layer of marinated meat covered with damp banana leaves, on top of that fava beans in their pods, corn and tamales, more herbs. It is then covered by a tarp, weighted by earth, and served a few hours later. Cooking underground pays homage to Pachamama, the Earth Mother.

Only a few were invited for lunch, and it was then that Lourdes started talking to Nicky, who, being curious, had gravitated to her table. Afterwards she asked me if it would be alright to take him out with her group in the afternoon, and I said yes. I didn't ask where they were going. It had never occurred to me that she would take him with her into town as part of an official visit, and later to a meeting at the town hall. So, I never made arrangements to bring him home if he got restless.

As Nicky was leaving with her entourage, some of the hotel staff came out to see them off. They were surprised she was taking Nicky. They joked with her saying that he could be the beginning of the end of her political career, but she joked back saying, "I have already lost the election." Everyone there was pro-Lourdes. "Poor Lourdes," they said as she waved goodbye, "she has no idea what she's in for."

We waited hours for them to return. None of us knew where they were, and the longer they were gone the more Pisco Sours we consumed and the wilder became our speculation. When they returned, Nicky ran to our table and one of her team was sent over to tell us about their day. She told us, "Nicky walked with Lourdes Flores through town, holding her hand and greeting people. He enjoyed the crowds and the cheering, but after the walk they went to a meeting at the Town Hall, and that's when things went terribly wrong." Nicky was put next to her at the main table. And when the initial excitement wore off, he was asked to sit quietly; and he got bored and started wandering around the room. When the mayor saw the empty seat next to her he quickly seized the opportunity to talk with Lourdes on his own. However, when Nicky saw someone had taken his seat, he took hold of the mayor's shirt and pulled hard saying: "Get up, that's my place!" When they bribed him with sweets and caffeinated soda he got worse.

By the time they brought him back he was bouncing off the walls from all the sugar and caffeine. Everyone from the group looked exhausted; as soon as they turned Nicky over to me they disappeared.

CHILDREN'S THEATRE

M any of Nicky's friends left Lima on weekends, or spent the time with their families, so I looked for ways to entertain him on my own. The local theatre hadn't changed much over the years. It smelled damp and musty, and looked long overdue for decoration. The productions were amateur but charming, and tickets were always available. Once we saw the Wizard of Oz. The Peruvian Dorothy didn't sing, she mimed and danced, but whatever her deficiencies in talent she made up for with her enthusiasm. The show had a character all of its own. Some of the roles were eliminated, and Toto was a man dressed as a dog with a painted face. But it worked! Dorothy only had seconds on stage before she was swept away by a tornado. She whirled across the stage like a dervish, through pumped-in steam and flashing lights, and then the theatre went pitch dark. When the lights came on you knew that Dorothy had landed in another place because the scenery had changed.

The audience was encouraged to participate in the performances, talking back and forth with the actors as in the old

Punch and Judy shows. This caused Nicky to become overexcited. I couldn't understand much of what he was saying, or if he was going too far, which I often feared he was. When the bad witch came on and demanded her sister's shoes back, all the children booed and shrieked in their high-pitched screams for her to go away. Nicky took an immediate dislike to the witch, leading the children in an unrelenting diatribe against her, hardly allowing her to speak. When the witch disappeared off stage the audience breathed a collective sigh of relief, but when she crept back in through the curtain behind Dorothy the children knew she was in trouble.

Nicky stood up and warned Dorothy: "Look behind you." Then he shouted: "Throw water at her!"

The bad witch, who was already furious with Nicky for the interruptions, stopped in mid-sentence and stormed over to the edge of the stage, this time addressing him directly: "How did you know about the water?"

He replied, "I saw it on television."

She shouted back, "You've ruined everything. That part wasn't supposed to be known until the end."

She then lifted the front of her skirt and began stamping her feet, mimicking frenzy. The audience went wild and Nicky, being on a high with all the chaos he had caused, offered: "Here, we can use this." Before I could stop him he shot up to the front of the stage to help Dorothy by throwing his bottle of Sprite on the witch. The witch shrieked and made the sign of the cross with her fingers, like a hex to keep him away.

I sunk lower into my seat. Dorothy rushed back on stage, just in time to throw a bucket of confetti on the witch, who vanished into the blackness lamenting: "There's no place like home."

It was an ordeal taking Nicky out on my own. I didn't speak the language and he did, which made me feel self-conscious and put me at a disadvantage. I was never sure what he was saying,

149

which was at times funny, but often not. It confused our roles, giving him control. I was dependent on a five year old for my voice. People talked directly to Nicky after they realized I couldn't speak Spanish, leaving me out of the conversation, which was empowering for so young and mischievous a child.

SUICIDE

During the week Nicky and I would wake early, and when he went down to catch the bus for school I would go with him and start walking at 6:45 a.m. After that the traffic built up, and so did the pollution.

I always followed the same route. I saw the same people, walked at the same pace and knew what to expect at every turn along the way. Except that this time, as I came around the corner and up to the main road, there was a crowd of people blocking the sidewalk. Accidents often happened at that junction, usually small rear-end collisions, because instead of yielding to the traffic, cars pushed their way out and other cars piled up behind them. When they were forced to brake sharply, they got clobbered from behind. Because of all the people I stepped off the sidewalk and went around them; and that's when I saw the body, covered with newspapers, except that her small white feet were sticking out at the end.

I imagined the person was hit crossing the road, until I bumped into a friend who told me: "No, the woman jumped from one of the apartments."

I shuddered to think that her body, which had been lying on the ground a few feet away, was still warm. I kept walking to clear my mind, and after more than an hour I came back around to the same place, never expecting to see the body again. An ambulance was waiting next to her, but because of all the official paperwork involved, the body couldn't be moved. She had landed outside the entrance of an apartment block where people were coming and going, and children were going past the building on their way to school. But her body remained where she jumped.

Her suicide haunted me. Maybe because she was a woman, close to my own age, and because I had seen her discarded body I felt her pain. I wondered what kind of despair caused her to lose all hope and prompted her to kill herself in that way. There was no chance to change her mind, no going back. It was brave, a final defiant act of freedom - choosing death as her ultimate solution and then fearlessly stepping out into the cold morning air, forever. The next morning, I passed her building on my usual route, but this time I was afraid. I worried that after such a violent death her spirit might have remained earthbound, unable to find peace and move on to another place, lingering where she had fallen; and then attach itself to me.

Later that week, I was driving to a party with friends. I hardly responded to the conversation. They asked, "Hey gringa, what's up?" I told them about the suicide and they said: "Yes, horrible, we saw it on the news. Her husband was a banker."

Salvador told me: "A lot of people jump," and as we passed a hotel he told me about a man who killed his lover there, by throwing her out the window. He said, "He had an argument with his girlfriend; they struggled and then he threw her out. He's still in jail." This wasn't the comfort I needed. She wouldn't have gone out willingly. There was time for him to change his mind. The thought repeated itself in my mind, a man picked up a woman and threw her to an agonising death, and possibly, only moments before, they had been lovers. At least the woman who jumped had chosen her fate. There was some comfort in that I suppose.

The next day I told the stories to a friend, who knew a man who jumped to his death in the atrium of the same hotel. Except that this man landed on the buffet table, next to several people having lunch. I listened in horror, and when my Spanish teacher arrived I couldn't concentrate on my books, and I began translating the stories I heard. Afterwards she told me about a man who jumped off another building in the centre of Lima and landed at the feet of a pedestrian who happened to be passing by. She told me: "The man who jumped died instantly, but the man on whose feet he landed went insane."

After that, she remembered another story of a man who jumped to his death and landed on the roof of a car, killing the young couple inside who were kissing goodnight.

None of these suicides made sense to me, especially in a Catholic country. I couldn't understand what problems could be worse than the threat of eternal damnation. My Catholic school taught me all about damnation, and it made a lasting impression on me. I dreaded the thought of my soul being stuck in a state of limbo, tormented for an eternity from which there was no escape. Salvador noticed my concern and told me: "Don't worry. If the person asks for forgiveness on the way down, and they're sincere, they will be saved."

I had to memorize parts of Hamlet in school, and they repeated in my head: "but the dread of something after death, the undiscovered country from whose bourn no traveller returns, puzzles the will and makes us rather bear those ills we have than fly to others that we know not of? Thus conscience does make cowards of us all." Shakespeare made perfect sense to me. Why would anyone cross into another life and risk the possibility of something worse at the other end?

When my teacher returned the following day, she remembered another story about a woman in Miraflores who jumped off a bridge that over-passed a busy road. As she jumped a truck loaded with bales of raw cotton passed underneath, the cotton broke her fall, and she survived. I'm sure the shock shortened the driver's life considerably, but the woman was fine. As far as people know, she is the only one who has ever survived jumping off the bridge, and for a short time she became a minor celebrity. During an interview, the woman swore she hadn't intended to kill herself. She told the reporter that the spirits had made her jump. She admitted they hadn't exactly pushed her, but they had coaxed her over the edge. I have been told that the spirits of the people who have died there possess the bridge. It is a notorious spot for suicides. At one time they posted a guard at one end to stop people from jumping, but he wasn't able to stop everyone, so as a last resort they have permanently enclosed the bridge in thick transparent plastic to keep people from going over the edge.

Several months after the suicide, Nicky and I were walking in the afternoon. We saw police cars and a fire truck outside an apartment building and a crowd of people in the street. Nicky asked a man, "Was there a fire?" He seemed embarrassed and pointed up toward the building. "Look." he said, "There is a man in one of the apartments trying to throw a woman out the window."

I wasn't sure I understood, but when I looked up I saw a woman bent backward out the window, clutching the curtains, struggling to pull herself in. I put my hand over Nicky's eyes, pulling him under my arm, half dragging him to get him out of there. I feared that any second she might fall, and that we would hear the dull thud of shattered flesh and bones as she hit the ground, and that we would never rid ourselves of that memory.

The woman was fighting for her life against this lunatic, with only the curtains to save her. There were witnesses. He wasn't going to get away with it, but no one could reach them. I struggled to make sense of what was happening. Was he psychotic, or was this proof that human sacrifice is genetically encoded in our DNA? Instead of throwing a young virgin off a mountain to appease the gods, he had to make do with what was available. Our brains have not evolved much since then.

Even a perceived threat causes a primitive physiological reaction, involuntarily flooding us with adrenaline, diverting blood to our extremities, and causing a flight or fight reaction to take over from reasoning. It gives us the best chance of survival and the way to pass our genes onto future generations. The gods must have cursed this blundering throwback, as his meagre offering clawed her way back in.

I read that in Chile during the 1960s, after their worst earthquake in recorded history, an uneducated farmer called Juan José Painecur and his friend were ordered by the local machi - the witchdoctor - to sacrifice Juan's five year old grandson, in order to appease the gods and to protect the village from further harm. They were told to cut off the child's arms and legs, and to bury his body at the edge of the sea, like a post. Their isolated village had been devastated, and then battered by aftershocks and a series of tsunamis, and being cut off from the outside world they had little left but their faith. The waves carried the child's body out into the ocean. They believed the witch doctor when he told them that sacrificing the child would save the village. For millennia primitive people have responded to catastrophes in this way. The men confessed to the crime and served two years in jail before being set free by a judge who ruled that they had acted without free will; driven by an irresistible natural force of ancestral tradition.

Sacrifice was a deep-rooted belief and was practiced in Peru until abolished by its Spanish conquerors and colonizers. Missionaries and priests came to convert the natives to Christianity, stamping out many of their customs and beliefs, including the human sacrifice which the Spanish deemed morally repugnant. Never mind all the references to sacrifice in the same Bible that they preached,

155

and that our God, who they were being coerced to believe in, had allowed his only son to be brutally sacrificed for our sins.

I only hoped that I was an inappropriate sacrifice. After all, their god demanded virgins and flawless youth. He might have thrown me back, showing his contempt. Nevertheless I find myself instinctively shying away from windows, and respectful not to say anything that could provoke the sacrificial need in the opposite sex.

THE BRUJA WITH SALVADOR

I hadn't seen my fortune-teller for some time, so I asked Salvador if he would ring her and make an appointment for me. He had heard about her through friends who waxed lyrical about her predictions, claiming that everything she told them came true. So, Salvador decided he would come with me and have his future read, but when he called to make our appointment he was told she was dead. The person who answered the phone appeared impatient to get rid of Salvador and would give no more information. The last time I saw her, she said she would tell me about a man I had dined with, but I had to wait until the next time we met. She said he was someone very important in my life. Now I would never know what she was going to say.

Salvador and I were psyched up to have our fortunes read, so we rang several friends hoping to find a replacement, but there was none with her reputation. We were given the name of a fortune-teller from a friend, but he didn't recommend her. I decided to go anyway, and Salvador offered to come with me and translate. The first thing she told me was that she dreamt that I was a priest standing on a mountain and that I had psychic powers. Years before, I had had a similar dream. I dreamt I was a healer on the top of a mountain wearing white robes. The dream made such an impression on me that I wrote it down and kept it.

She didn't have anything spectacular to tell me, but at some point, she turned to Salvador and said, "I can't help but pick up some things about you." She told him that a spirit had attached itself to him and that it was sapping his energy. He said he had heard this before, but so far no one had been able to rid him of it. At the end of the meeting she said I could ask three questions. I asked her about my love life, about my future, and my last question was about a friend who was having problems. She explained: "Someone has put a strong curse on your friend, and his situation looks dire."

I was desperate and asked: "Isn't there anything that can be done to help him?"

She replied: "Yes, for a nominal fee I can remove his curse through you."

Salvador was interested in exorcizing his bothersome spirit, so we made an appointment to come back together.

Salvador explained that the exorcism would take three appointments, and that it was expensive. When he picked me up the following week, I was curious to see two paper bags in the back of his car. They were bulging with eggs, quince, lemons, and tins of condensed milk. I asked him, "Salva, why have you brought these things?" That was when Salvador told me that the ceremony also included the fruit and standing naked while she poured milk mixed with herbs over our heads. Before then he told me it was he who would have to stand naked while she spat alcohol on him. I said: "To each his own."

He swore he had told me, but he hadn't. It wasn't the sort of thing I could forget. By now it was too late to back out. My friend was so grateful I was doing this for him that I didn't have the heart to tell him I'd cancel, just because I would have to stand naked in front of a total stranger while she rubbed fruits and eggs across my body, performing some form of witchcraft. He would have never believed me and thought it a lame excuse for cancelling at the last second.

We arrived early for our appointment and, while we were waiting, her maid came in and numbered our eggs with a ball point pen; three eggs for each of us. Starting with our number one egg she instructed us to put them under our left arm for three minutes, and the other two in sequence. Afterwards she numbered six of our lemons, three for each of us. When we finished with the eggs, we were to put the lemons under our arm, one at a time for three minutes each. The last item to be put under our arm was the quince. She handed us a timer and left.

It was impossible to sit with an egg under my arm and not laugh. This set Salvador off, and once we started laughing neither of us could stop. The more we laughed, the more we worried about breaking the egg under our arm, which caused us to laugh uncontrollably.

I was the first to be called in, and the fortune-teller told me to take off my clothes and step into the shower, which had been jury-rigged at the far end of her room. Goosebumps followed her hand as she ran the eggs one at a time up and down my legs. She slid them up my back, and down across my chest, and then she repeated the pattern with the lemons and quince. I stood there, shivering and sliding my toes back and forth on the slimy floor, thinking of Athlete's Foot and "Oh what a good friend I am." She rang bells, she hit sticks together, she made signs of the cross, and then she poured cold milk over my head. Afterwards she dropped a couple of thin paper napkins on the table for me to dry with.

After I had dressed, she brought Salvador in to translate. I watched as she broke my eggs into three glasses of water to read their shapes. The first egg she opened was milky, as if it had been slightly poached, but the other two eggs looked normal, except that one contained a small speck of blood. She studied the eggs at length and told me: "A strong curse was put on your friend. Someone put a potion in his food or drink. The curse was unquestionably the work of a professional."

I was told to wait in the other room while Salvador went through the ceremony. I could hear the chimes and the bells, and laughed out loud, visualizing him in the shower. My heart went out to Salvador. I knew he must be desperate to get rid of that spirit to stand naked in front of a woman he didn't know in a cold room. It wouldn't enhance his "penis with a hundred names", which I feared would retreat along with the troubling spirit the second she drenched him in cold milk.

After he got dressed I was called in while the fortune-teller read his eggs. They looked normal compared to mine. Which was a bit of a blow because if it wasn't a spirit causing his problems, then what was it?

She instructed us to go home and put our lemons on a fork and blacken them over a candle. We were told to take the blackened lemons seven blocks from the house, and, at a corner, throw them over our left shoulder. She cautioned: "Don't look back. It's bad luck to see them once you throw them." We were also told to put our quinces under our beds; and not to sleep with anyone until the cleansing was completed.

We arrived at my flat to blacken our lemons and headed straight to the kitchen for forks and candles. Afterwards we went to my bedroom and locked the door. I didn't want the maids to see what we were up to. They are superstitious, and I worried that they might quit if they thought we were practising some sort of black magic in the flat. Salvador told me: "Don't be stupid. If you bring a Peruvian man to your bedroom, it is for one reason. You have rushed back to have sex."

I said: "Don't flatter yourself! You're so immature, they would think I brought you home for your nap."

We felt like school children, hiding, up to something, whispering and holding our lemons over the flame. Every time we looked at each other we convulsed with laughter. When we finished blackening the lemons, we dropped them back in the bag and drove off, looking to find a corner where we could throw them. Lima is crowded with millions of people, on foot, in cars, riding bicycles, and every time we thought we had found the perfect corner to toss the lemons, someone would appear, so we would run back to the car and start driving again.

The next day was much the same, except the fortune-teller seemed happy that my eggs were clear. On the last day I couldn't go with Salvador because I had a party at Nicky's school, so he finished on his own and promised to translate for me the following day. As we entered her sitting room, we saw my lemons, eggs and quince all numbered and ready for me on the table, except that this time there were two other people in the room. We had never encountered anyone there before, and they surprised us.

I nonchalantly put the first egg under my arm, but as soon as I did Salvador nudged me with his knee and tilted his head in their direction, which set me into helpless laughter. Every time I would stop Salvador would lift an eyebrow and we would begin laughing again. They were embarrassed when we showed up. One began fidgeting with her cell phone, flipping it over with her thumb until it slipped and fell to the floor between them. They glanced at us from time to time, and then huddled closer together so we couldn't hear what they were saying. Both of them seemed ready to change their minds and run, but before they could decide what to do the fortune-teller came in and whisked them off to the other room.

When we heard her clicking the sticks and ringing bells Salvador and I became hysterical. We laughed so loud, I'm certain they could hear us. I worried she was going to come in and tell us to leave, and that I wouldn't be allowed to complete the ceremony, but to my great relief she never came. Next it was my turn to go in. Her room wasn't heated, and I shivered as I stepped into the cold slimy shower, grateful that this was the end. After she finished, I got dressed and she returned with Salvador to examine my eggs. She was pleased they were clear. "Hallelujah!" the process was complete my friend was saved.

We went home to blacken my lemons and then to search for a corner to throw them, which caused me to be late meeting my date for lunch. My hair was damp and I smelled of herbs and the sweet milky smell of a baby. Worse, I hadn't time to reapply make-up or wipe away the black mascara that had run in rivers down my cheeks from laughing so much. But I didn't care. I knew he wasn't right for me, even before the fortune-teller had told me. She didn't like him, she felt he contaminated those around him with his negative energy, and she had advised me to get rid of him straight away. When I hesitated to follow her counsel, after all he was fun, and he liked good whiskey and restaurants, she told me that he was a latent homosexual. Neither Salvador nor I could contain our amusement at what she said, but she just shrugged us off and told us: "Even he isn't aware of it yet."

The following week, we went to throw away our quinces. But while we were looking for a corner to throw them, I noticed that mine was covered in a thick hairy black mould, whereas Salvador's quince looked fresh. This didn't seem right and I asked Salvador to ring the fortune-teller. She told him to have me return at once. I needed to start right away, no charge. That was the last thing I wanted. I had a million things to do before I left for London. She was fully booked but she was adamant I come, and of her own volition she shuffled her appointments around to fit me in, so I grudgingly agreed to start again.

This time Salvador couldn't come with me to translate and I talked Ken, a Scottish friend who spoke Spanish, into coming. Again, there was someone in the waiting room when we arrived, but I didn't laugh. Ken felt self-conscious being there, and he made no attempt to conceal his embarrassment. After the woman was called to the other room, Ken got up and looked around. Across the hall he spotted a life sized photograph of my fortune-teller next to what appeared to be a ghost. He told me: "This is a trick of light. The photo is a fake. Muffi come here and look at this, she's a charlatan." I told him: "Who cares? I am doing this for a friend. Relax for heaven's sake." But he was miserable.

The fortune-teller took me to her room and waited outside while I undressed. I knew the routine by now, and stepped into the slimy shower and called her in. When she finished the ceremony, Ken was called in to translate. My eggs were clear which puzzled her. She read my coca leaves and told my fortune: "Soon you will meet the love of your life. You are destined for great joy and wonderful things. Your future lover is foreign, maybe Swiss. You will meet him soon, maybe at a party in Lima with friends. He is passionate and you will spend a great deal of time in bed."

She was very enthusiastic and descriptive about our lovemaking, concluding that my soon-to-be-lover was particularly skilled in something which Ken blatantly refused to translate. That was not the type of personal detail he had cared to hear about, and he stumbled awkwardly over the rest of the translation. The last thing she told me was, "When the stock market rallies in June, get out, because after that it will drop like a stone." Then, as we were leaving she remembered the quince, and told me to take it to London and sleep with it under my bed. This was the first time I had seen Ken smile since we arrived. He knew it would be impossible for me to take it through customs. Fruit is contraband, and he relished the situation. I said: "Tell her that it is illegal for me to bring into England, I can't do it." In any case I couldn't imagine walking around Chelsea with a quince, but as my eggs were clear, she agreed that it could wait under my bed in Lima until I returned.

There was something odd about the way she studied me as we were leaving the room. Something was left unsaid. I could see she was still baffled by my quince, because my eggs were clear. Then she knew. She told me: "Someone has made your quince turn black. It wasn't you. Whoever was in your bed you must get rid of him at once. You would be wise to put baskets of lemons and quinces in all the corners of your apartment, and garlic to repel his energy."

And sweeping the air with her hand, she cleared away the last traces of his presence.

HOTEL DE LA BORDA

Quique often invited Nicky and me to come for the weekend when he drove to Nasca on business. He liked our company, and he knew that at a moment's notice we could be ready to go. We took the road south along the coast to Paracas, and then headed inland across miles and miles of desert. The roads through some of the smaller towns appeared to have evolved from donkey trails, rather than being planned professionally. There were sharp, unexpected turns, and steep drops to houses below. Quique had travelled the same route since he was a child, and he knew the journey by heart. Sometimes he became nostalgic as we drove, and recounted stories about Nasca, which included pointing out every place en route where he had lost family and friends in car accidents.

The entrance of the hotel isn't imposing, but once you pass through the gates the startling richness of colour is dramatic, especially after driving through miles of desert. Gnarled vines of Bougainvillea, their stems as thick as trees, climb the front of the house and fan out across the roof, culminating in such an extravagant excess of flowers that there isn't enough space; and they tumble down, spilling their fiery colour over the edge. The hacienda is painted colonial red, with white trim surrounding green doors and shutters. Its landscape is as old as the hacienda, which gives the feeling of permanence, and that everything belongs just where it is.

In the gardens they kept caged birds, a family of peacocks, and two llamas tied under trees. Nicky swam and played with his friends, while I sat in the garden and read. We always requested the room at the end of the passageway, near Quique's room. It didn't have the best view, but it had an adjoining room with a large window at the back overlooking fields and a dirt road. "Don't leave anything near the window," the Porter always reminded us. "Thieves have reached in through the metal bars of the window with poles, and hooked out cameras and clothes."

We loved the soundless pitch-black nights, nights which were so dark that you had to run your hands along the wall to find the light switch if you needed to get up for the loo. We gorged on mangos and avocados fresh from the trees, and platters stacked full of just-picked asparagus dripping with butter.

Quique used his driver for the trip, leaving space in the car for neither Spot nor Nicky's nanny. Nicky knew his way around the hotel by then and everyone there knew Nicky, telling me: "Don't worry. He's fine, we will keep an eye on him." He had made friends with the children whose families worked for Quique. They were used to Nicky running in and out of their houses. Everyone tended to keep an eye on each others' children, and while Nicky was with them I knew he would keep out of mischief and be safe. But he wasn't always in their company. At some point, he lured the family of peacocks into the drawing room with bread and then slammed the door shut behind them. They took flight in survival mode, circling the room and shitting the walls at eye level, frantically trying to escape. It was a new challenge for the staff, who had to get the birds out safely and clean up the mess.

The next day I had lunch with Quique and his family, but I was nervous having Nicky out of sight and not knowing where he was. I asked, "Has anyone seen Nicky?" They told me: "Don't worry gringa, relax, he's fine." All the same, I couldn't relax and I went looking for him, as Nicky was without his nanny to follow him around and protect him. I also worried because the people working at the hotel were used to their own children, who had grown up in the country. They knew to stay away from stray dogs, animals, rusty nails, open wells, machinery and all the other hazards that Nicky, who had grown up in the city, had never encountered before. I found him behind a hedge, not far from where we were having lunch. He was playing quietly by himself and had just diverted all the water that runs through the grounds of the hotel and supplies water to the irrigation systems of several other farms in the area. They had once been part of the same estate and the water supply was still connected.

When I found Nicky the water was rising and had started to overflow the irrigation channel. I had to jump across onto a small concrete platform in order to crank the floodgate back up. The mechanism was stiff, and difficult for me to open. I don't know how he had the strength to close it by himself. He hadn't removed the wooden handle, which was the saving grace, so I was able to crank it back up before any real damage was done.

When I returned to the table, my trousers dripping wet, I explained what had happened. They joked, "Don't worry gringa, we're insured." Nevertheless after that everyone took a keen interest in Nicky's whereabouts. They often checked on him themselves, or sent employees to see where he was.

So I knew he was safe.

NIGHTCLUB QUIQUE

Quique and I were invited to hear Juan, a musician and friend, playing piano at a local club. The performance started late, so Quique agreed to meet at my flat for a snack and a drink before going. When Quique arrived I wasn't ready, so Quique fixed a drink and talked with Nicky while I got dressed. It wasn't until we were going out the door that we realized neither of us had kept the invitation and we didn't know the address. I had a vague idea of where it was. Quique told me: "Come on, let's go. Once we get into the general area, we can ask someone. It won't be difficult to find a club."

As we were leaving I remembered the quince under my bed, and that it was time to throw it away. Quique told me: "You must be joking! You're not bringing that rotten thing in my car!" I put it inside two plastic bags and said, "I am not leaving without it!"

When we got close to where we thought the club should be we stopped at a restaurant. Quique asked the doorman for directions to the club, but he hadn't heard of it so Quique went inside to find someone who could help. We were badly parked and I waited in the car. Ten minutes later, Quique emerged surrounded by friends. They kissed me hello and gave us directions, and said that they were also going to the concert. We kissed goodbye and set off to meet them at the club.

I reminded Quique about my quince, but he joked, "You don't really believe in that rubbish, do you?" He pulled alongside a dustbin and he told me to drop it in.

I told him: "Are you crazy? I'm not about to take any chances by not following her instructions. There's no way I am going through that ceremony again."

The streets were overflowing with people. I was afraid to throw the quince and have someone run after me to give it back, because once it was thrown it was bad luck to see it again. We found the only parking space left, which was directly in front of the club. Quique tipped the doorman and told him: "Watch the car. We will be back in a moment, we have something to do before we go in."

As we were searching for a corner to throw my quince a maître d' saw us and ran over to give us a copy of his menu. His restaurant was new and virtually empty, so he was all over Quique, trying to persuade him to bring me in for supper. Quique asked me in English: "Did you throw it?" I replied: "No. How can I throw it in front of the maître d'?" He said: "Okay, I'll distract him." And they both turned around, facing the restaurant. Quique was making all sorts of extravagant gestures, gestures which were so exaggerated that he attracted the attention of the security guard and some people further up the street. We didn't look like criminals, but it was obvious we were up to something.

Quique asked me again: "Did you throw it?" I told him: "No, this isn't a good place. Look at all the people. And because of you every one of them is staring at us."

When we got to the next corner, there was a small tree, which provided a tiny cover. I thought, "It's now or never," and I threw the bag over my shoulder and ran. Quique turned and ran after me, laughing and panting to keep up.

The concert was nearly over by the time we went in, and when Quique realized how little time there was left, he insisted on bargaining down the entrance fee. He tried every trick, but they wouldn't budge, which delayed even us further. There was no longer space at the table with our friends, so we were taken past them like truant children and put in a far corner overlooking the stage. It was a lively performance, and as the evening quickly came to an end we blamed each other for arriving late. We had hardly had time to settle in and finish our drinks before it was time to kiss everyone goodbye and go home. After leaving the club we found ourselves caught in the midst of heavy weekend traffic; locking car doors, creeping defensively through traffic lights, dodging cars, honking horns, screeching brakes, and avoiding pedestrians dashing across the street just when they were least expected. In the end I was grateful that fate had shortened our time at the club and that Quique's reflexes had remained razor sharp for the drive home. As I was stepping out of the car he asked, "You don't really believe in that nonsense about the quince, do you?"

I answered: "Maybe not about the quince, but there are many things that I don't understand. So why take risks."

LIVING IN PERU

An American friend once criticized me by saying: "Nicky is not being brought up in the real world growing up in Peru. The people working for you spoil him too much." This was ironic, because one of the reasons that I loved living in Lima was because it reminded me of my childhood. Growing up in Florida during the fifties was idyllic. We had live-in help and everything was taken care of for us. Now all of that has changed, whereas in Peru much of that lifestyle has remained the same.

Nicky did everything for himself when we went to visit my mother. He adapted to the different lifestyles as easily as he switches between languages. Only once, when we were leaving for Florida, did he ask: "Mummy what will we do without Armandina to cook for us?" I missed her too. I love good food, but I can't cook. I told him: "Part of the Florida adventure is learning to make your own bed and surviving grandma's cooking."

I never understood the American obsession with independence. All this "Do it yourself". If I have a choice of doing something myself or having someone to do it for me, I will always choose the latter. Why would I want to be independent from someone who cooks and cleans for me?

I once read about an experiment in the United States where a doctor wired several mothers to a monitor to check their stress levels throughout the day. He wanted to compare their stress levels to that of executives in high-powered positions, and with professionals who had high-risk occupations, such as floor traders, racing drivers and professional athletes. All sorts of professions were monitored, but he didn't find one that produced the same continuous level of stress as that suffered by a mother looking after a child under five years of age; and having two children under five was worse. I cannot deal with that kind of stress.

Parents in the States learn through the news all the dangers of leaving their precious child with a childminder, who often might be someone they didn't know, or an inexperienced teenager. So for peace of mind they take their children with them everywhere they go, usually glued to a tablet or a phone. The children hardly look up, and they rarely speak. Electronic gadgets keep them quiet and entertained, but over-stimulated, unimaginative and inarticulate; which is not how I wanted Nicky to grow up.

Nicky was living in the real world. He wasn't abandoned in front of an electronic screen, showing a Hollywood version of life. We were surrounded by reality. He could see that not everyone succeeded or owned a home, and that people died in tragic ways. Life wasn't sanitized and glossed over. He met people who were rich and others who had nothing. All Nicky had to do was to spend an hour in the kitchen to realize that we were not all born with the same privileges or advantages, and that life isn't necessarily fair or simple. He also saw people who cared, and who looked out for each other. We lived a wonderful life in Lima and anyone who has spent time there doesn't want to leave.

NICKY'S NANNY IN LIMA.

Nicky's first nanny in Lima was young, with no children of her own. She was reliable but impatient, and often overwhelmed by his behaviour. As a means of keeping him under control, she tried using religion. Probably the same as my Catholic school had done to frighten me. My teacher often warned me: "Naughty children don't go to heaven." But at the same time, she told me that because I wasn't Catholic I had no chance of redemption, which was counterproductive. I was doomed, condemned to go with the rest of the infidels when I died, and it sure as hell wasn't going to be to heaven.

I told Nicky: "If someone threatens you will be punished by God, tell me. It isn't true." But Nicky always challenged me asking, "What about The Flood and Noah's Ark? God punished everyone, including children. He drowned them." I told him, "Yes, but that was a long time ago, He hasn't done it since. God doesn't give up on people so easily. Think about it. If He killed everyone who was a little naughty, or who had made a mistake, there would be no one left for Him to redeem. It would be counterproductive."

Religion and superstition play a large part in Peruvian life, and I was often at a loss to explain. One day Nicky came home from school and told me, "If children are naughty an elf will draw a cross on their hand while they are asleep and they will die." It reminded me a bit of the bogeyman, which was used to frighten me when I was young. I believe he was supposed to carry us off if we were naughty, and not murder us. However, sometimes it was difficult to tell, it depended on how angry the person was. I told Nicky: "Elves only exist in fairy tales. They are small and cute, with pointed ears. They are not monsters lurking in the shadows waiting to draw crosses on the hands of sleeping children to kill them." After our talk, he seemed reassured, but seconds later he rang everyone we knew in Lima to make certain that Peruvian elves didn't maintain different customs than the ones I was familiar with. When he finished talking to my friends he seemed satisfied and then went on to the next thing. It was complicated to explain to Nicky that the people who worked for us believed in certain superstitions and that others with a higher education perhaps saw things differently. Spending time in the kitchen and on the school bus, he heard all sorts of stories.

One time Nicky came to my bedroom and told me: "Mummy, if you go to the desert in Peru and see a baby on the ground, throw a rock at its head."

I said: "What! Who in the hell told you that?" But I suspected who it was.

He explained to me: "The babies on the ground in the desert are really ghosts or spirits that trick you into coming over in order to take away your memory."

I told him: "That is ridiculous."

He said, "Suit yourself. But don't say I didn't warn you; not that you would remember who I was if you didn't have a memory." He added, "If you see a baby sitting on its mother's lap don't throw a stone at its head because it's probably real. Only the ones on the ground at night are illusions. And don't follow a Vicuña into a cave. They can trick you and take away your memory!"

I started teasing him saying, "Uh oh, I knew I should have never followed that Vicuña. Who are you? Why are you in my room?" Some of his stories did get a little over the top. But I only heard Nicky's interpretation of the story. Children love to frighten each other. He probably heard the scariest stories through his friends.

SHOPPING

Nicky and I were walking to the shop when we saw Mutti, a friend of mine's mother, being pushed in a wheelchair. She had always been my saviour at large parties and family gatherings, going out of her way to keep me company when she saw me struggling with Spanish, or standing lost and miserable on my own. I knew that she had been in hospital, and I wanted to say hello and introduce her to Nicky, who she hadn't met. She smiled as we approached and told us, "I am only in this wheelchair because I have just left the hospital. Everything is fine now. I am alright, but I have no recollection of going to the hospital. I don't remember much of what has happened during the past few days, which upsets me."

I told her: "Your memory will come back, it takes time. Your thinking obviously isn't affected. I would have never known you had been ill, from talking to you. You look great."

She told us: "Yes, I feel fine, but I am concerned that my memory will never come back to being as good as it was. It frightens me to have forgotten so much."

I could see that she wanted to talk, and I was grateful that Nicky was being quiet and empathetic. When she started to look tired we kissed goodbye, and her nurses took her home. Nicky looked concerned; he gently tugged on my sleeve. I bent down, and he whispered, "Mummy, do you think she followed a Vicuña?"

For years, every time Nicky and I got into a taxi, he would ask the driver if he believed in ghosts. We have listened to many of their stories. The most famous ghost they told us about is the one that haunts La Casa Matusita in the centre of Lima. We have detoured past the house many times to take a look, hoping to catch a glance of a shadowy figure peering down at us from the upstairs window so as to settle our dispute about ghosts once and for all. Do they exist? The top of the house where the ghost is supposed to haunt is now a burnt out shell and the ground floor is a shop that sells appliances. Nowadays there is nothing eerie or mysterious about it. Once there were rumours that a huge cash reward would be given to anyone who could stay upstairs alone for the entire night, but no one has collected the reward, because, according to the legend, everyone who has stayed the night in the house has either died or gone insane.

There is gossip that the Americans fabricated the rumour of the ghost, because the room it is supposed to haunt overlooked the former American Embassy and they didn't want someone in there spying on them. Others say the rumour is rubbish.

Nicky doesn't believe in ghosts. I do. As a teenager, I lived with one in London. It haunted my bedroom, and if I didn't sleep with the lights on it would come over to my bed and exhale heavily in my ear, frightening me half to death. No one believed me about the ghost, so while I was away my mother put her guest in my bedroom without broaching the subject. Her friend must have turned out the light when she went to bed. Her screams in the middle of the night gave Mummy pause to reconsider my oft repeated grievance about the ghost.

At least half the taxi drivers Nicky questioned told him that they had seen a ghost. One driver patted the seat next to him and said, "Normally the ghost of a young boy accompanies me while

I work. He is five or six years old, but for some reason he hasn't shown up today." This was a bit of a relief for me.

Another driver told us he hadn't believed in ghosts until recently when he had picked up a woman. He said, "It was a long drive to her house and we were talking, but as we passed a graveyard she fell silent. When I looked into my rear view mirror she had disappeared from the back of my car without a trace."

On another trip, the driver told us that his brother came to see him in the middle of the night, but half his body was missing. His mother woke him in the morning, with the news that his brother had been killed in a car crash, that night.

Once we got a very old driver, who endlessly pondered Nicky's question about ghosts, searching into some deep crevice in his brain for the long-lost information. We had nearly forgotten Nicky had asked him a question when he responded: "Yes, I believe in ghosts." Though he added, he hadn't actually seen a ghost, but he was almost certain he had heard one singing in a graveyard. "It sounded as if it might have been drunk."

Nicky has a different understanding of Peru than I have because he speaks the language. He talked to all sorts of different people and he never stopped asking questions, whereas I mostly talked with people who spoke English, which implies a more rarefied education. Also, because Nicky was a child, people were less inhibited when they spoke to him. Nicky was always interested in everything around him, and because of his curiosity he got to know more about people and their different customs than most other children of his age.

THE BEGGAR

Nicky looked forward to Halloween. Every year our local grocery got into the spirit, dressing a few employees like witches and ghouls to hand out candies and treats. Shelves full of sweets were draped with spiders' webs and loaded with blood-coloured candies, Dracula teeth, plastic gravestones, and all the spooky Halloween decorations that children love.

As soon as Nicky returned from school we left for the store. We walked the five or six blocks to get there, and just before we reached the entrance of the shop we found an old woman begging. She was short, stocky, and wearing a bowler style hat with a small rim that barely shaded her face. Her clothes were traditional Andean dress: a heavy short full skirt, a colourful shawl, and hair worn pulled back tightly into two long greyish black braids. She held out her hand as we approached, and then brought her fingers up to her mouth and together. Nicky signalled me, I nodded, and he quickly reached into his pocket and gave her money.

Nicky and I split up as we entered the store. He headed for the candy aisle while I shopped for groceries. After I had gotten everything on my list, I found Nicky near the checkout counter, struggling to carry a bag topped by a plastic pumpkin. I had given him money to buy Halloween candy for himself and his friends, but he was beaming as he told me: "Mummy, look, I got this for the old woman begging."

He bought her the plastic pumpkin together with a huge bag of candies, potato chips, a carton of chocolate milk and a Coca-Cola. I wondered what her reaction would be and only hoped that she would be as excited as he was about his gifts. When we went outside, she was still in the same place. Nicky went over to her while I waited near the entrance. I watched as she slowly took the pumpkin from his hands and then lifted it towards the sky as if to give thanks for the miracle she had just received. Then she clung to it. Perhaps she was afraid to let it go for fear that he was so young he might change his mind and take it back, or that she had misunderstood and it wasn't meant for her in the first place. Afterwards, he gave her the candy and explained that she should put it in the pumpkin and sell it to earn money during Halloween. She was so overwhelmed by the gifts that at first she didn't seem to grasp what he said. Maybe she only understood Quechua. She continued rocking back and forth clinging to the pumpkin, and every now and then she looked up and said something to the sky. He had the good sense to wait before giving her the other things.

I had never expected such a reaction and worried that the surprise of his gift might have been too much for her. Afterward she put everything on her skirt that was spread on the ground around her, and she touched them one by one, keeping them close as if to cherish and protect them. After a while, she reached over to Nicky and took his soft little hands and pressed them to her lips and gently kissed them, thanking him over and over again. It was very emotional and we waited until she settled down before we felt comfortable to leave her and go home. I was touched by Nicky's generosity and by her response. I had never before been witness to anything like that kind of joy or gratitude from receiving a gift, no matter how spectacular the gift had been, and I felt humbled by the lesson.

The next day, Nicky dragged me back to the store to see if she was still there. He told me: "Mummy, let's check and see if she needs more candy or something to eat." We looked everywhere, but she was nowhere in sight. He asked, "Mummy, where do you think she is?" I knew he was disappointed not to find her, and I didn't want to say that security had probably run her away. So I fibbed and told him, "She must have sold all the candy, and now she has enough money to retire and move to Miami. We will probably never see her again." He laughed as I described her in Miami Beach, wearing light colourful cotton clothes and floppy hats, going to the mall or sitting in her air-conditioned condo, and watching her telenovelas - soap operas.

But in reality, I knew that the poor old woman he was talking about was in fact probably close to my own age, and that her life was anything but fun.

THE EARTHQUAKE 2003

W e were waiting for the doorbell to ring, telling us that the car had arrived to take Peter to the airport. Nicky was begging: "Papi please don't go! Papi, stay!" Peter was hugging him, telling him that he would be back in a few weeks, but Nicky was inconsolable.

I bent down to pick Nicky up and as I did so my legs felt wobbly, as if I were about to faint. As I straightened up I realized it wasn't me that was shaking, it was the room. We were having an earthquake. The paintings were bouncing against the walls and the windows were pinging, sounding as if they were about to explode. All around us things were falling over and crashing to the floor. Nicky rushed over and pressed his face against the window to see what was happening outside, but Peter ran over and carried him back to the centre of the room. We were huddled together next to the lift. Neither of us knew what to do. The maids were in the kitchen crying. All of us were wondering: "Is this it? Is this the end?"

Nicky and I had been through several tremors before. They usually happened at night when we were asleep and we were woken by the motion or by friends ringing, checking to see we were all right. This earthquake was much stronger than the others, and it didn't let up. We were trapped on the seventh floor of a concrete building that was shaking as if attached to a giant jackhammer, as was everything in it. It was also making noises as if it were breaking up. I had no idea if our building had been designed to withstand earthquakes of this strength. Peru is on a fault line and earthquakes and tremors are common, you expect them, but they trigger a primordial fear of extinction and mutilation, and we never got used to them.

It wasn't all that long ago when I saw on the news the devastation after an earthquake in Turkey, leaving thousands dead. I watched rescuers sifting through the wreckage, some using their bare hands, while others used picks and mechanical diggers. It was a fight against time to find survivors. Family and friends were stranded outside, their town in ruins. People were praying for a miracle from the same God who had just destroyed their village and thrown them in the street, but they showed no loss of faith and there was little else they could do except pray. I was terrified we were going to share their fate, because until that moment I wouldn't have believed that a building could shake so violently on its foundations and not crumble.

When the ground moves beneath you, nowhere feels safe. It brings home how powerless we are against the forces of nature. Perhaps one more violent shake and ours would be a swift and violent end. I had expected the government to declare a state of emergency, and shut down the airport, but minutes later the Porter rang to say the car had arrived. Nicky and I went down to say goodbye and watched in silence as Peter's car pulled out into the traffic and accelerated down the street. We waited outside with the other residents, none of us knowing what to do next; people huddled together away from the buildings, hoping for a signal or a sign that it was safe to return. But when none came, Nicky and I decided we had waited long enough and we headed inside.

Some of the others followed our example and squeezed into the lift with us; maybe thinking that there was safety in numbers or that we were the sign it was safe to go in. It truly was a case of "the blind leading the blind". As we rode up I prayed that the earth was at peace, especially now that we were trapped in the lift with so many terrified people, knowing they would go berserk if the light flickered or failed and the building started shaking while we were trapped together in our metal cage.

NICKY WANTS TO RUN AWAY

On March 10th, 2000, Nasdaq peaked, but then fell 78% in the following months. After the tech bubble burst, my shares plummeted. I tried to remain optimistic about the economy and my investments, but our losses were always at the back of my mind. My portfolio was cut by more than sixty percent, and after a while I could no longer convince myself that our finances were just passing through a bad phase. The bank was in charge of my investments, and over the past two years they lost us so much money that, after we paid their fees, we were left with barely enough to live on. We should have gone back to Florida while I got my finances in order, but I didn't know what to do or where to turn for help, and I was terrified of making things worse. So I started praying for a miracle, instead of doing the obvious thing, like changing banks.

I sat hour after hour in front of the television, watching the stock market rising and falling, feeling more and more helpless. My friends could tell which way the market closed by my face. I withdrew to my room, watching financial reports in the hope that by listening to the experts their knowledge would suddenly manifest itself in me and that I too would become an expert. After another huge drop in the market Nicky came home from school and saw me watching the results come in. He said: "That's it ... I've had enough! I'm leaving. Every time I come home from school you're in one of your bad moods from watching the stock market." Then he went off and packed his suitcase with toys, a couple of books, and packets of potato chips, and sent Armandina down to storage to get Spot's travelling cage.

When Nicky was packed and ready to leave, Armandina came in and said: "Señora Muffi, he wants me to come and work for him. What do you want me to do? He told me: "I need you more than my mother does. She can keep Nancy, the other maid.""

I told her: "Well, he will need you for crossing the street and to help carry the luggage." We both agreed Nicky was very practical.

She was desperate for advice. I thought for a moment and then I went to find Nicky. He was waiting for Armandina by the lift, surrounded by his luggage, with Spot already in his cage. I apologised and asked him to stay. He knew he was in a strong bargaining position and said, "Okay, but there is one condition. You have to promise to stop watching the market from now or I'm leaving!"

I told him: "Alright "No news is good news."" Then he went off with Armandina to play. Our move to Peru with all its complicated arrangements had gone without incident. Life was good, but my optimism was short lived. We had arrived in Lima without a care in the world, then the dot com bubble burst, the bottom fell out of the stock market and the dollar devalued, causing our situation to change for the worse, almost overnight.

I tried to keep everything the same on the surface, we didn't move to a smaller place and I didn't lay anyone off. But I was terrified. I took fewer trips to London and I cut back on outings with friends; every unexpected expense overwhelmed me. I didn't explain why I had dropped out. That would have been the greatest humiliation: to be pitied. And worse, having to listen to endless advice.

Grandma's photo sits on my desk, her essence captured in an old sepia print from around 1911. She looks regal, gazing tenderly down at her daughter, a babe in arms, with my father seated next to her. She is dressed in fine white linen and lace, wearing a diamond and pearl necklace against a tight bodice, feminine perfection of a bygone age. I would have loved to be there with her, wrapped in her long starched skirts, unafraid and certain of who I was. She gave me a diamond necklace, which sat gathering dust in the safe. But instead of selling it, the sensible thing to do, I kept it. It was a reminder of when my privileged life seemed inalienable and I couldn't part with such an irreplaceable treasure. Grandma placed a note in the box saying: "Think of your Gammo when you wear this and how much she loves you," and I did. I was happy knowing it was there.

It also felt good to remember that my life wasn't always in such a mess.

LECTURE

Susy rang to tell me Deepak Chopra was coming to Lima, to give a lecture the following week. She was heading out now to buy tickets and told me: "If you want to come with me, I'll pick you up." I thought it was a miracle when she said that he was coming. In my mind, he was sent as an answer to my prayers. I was convinced that he was bringing me a message.

We got to the lecture early to secure good seats and ended up waiting hours for it to begin; there were interminable technical problems. Something went wrong with the sound system, which meant that they had to rewire the speakers, and the man who was translating had to be brought out and stand next to Deepak Chopra on stage. Even after all the complications and delays, his enthusiasm was contagious. He began by telling us that these hardships and inconveniences are great lessons. He emphasised this point by telling us a story about a problem he had had in London when all the phones in his suite went dead, before the era of cellular phones. Instead of getting frustrated and wasting time complaining to management, he went outside to use a public phone. Red phone boxes were ubiquitous in London at that time. They were about the size of a sentry box, but fully enclosed and covered from top to bottom in glass panes. As it was cold outside the warmth of his body and breath caused the window panes to steam up. Using his finger, he rubbed a tiny peephole to look out, and just outside was the woman he was trying to reach by phone. What had appeared to be a difficulty with the phones had actually been a blessing.

Nothing like that ever happened to me. When things went wrong they usually got a lot worse, not better. He told us: "We choose our destiny." Everything he said made sense, and maybe he was right. But if we do choose our destiny why would I have chosen mine? And if I did, I've changed my mind. I now choose brilliant, rich and sexy.

We had nothing in common to connect us, other than that I read his books. I sent him telepathic messages: "How can you be so certain that all my hardships are such fabulous lessons unless you have the courage to trade places with me and experience them for yourself?" I exhausted myself sending messages like: "I am in the audience. Look for me. If I have chosen this karma like you say I have, help me to send it back. You must feel that I am here, concentrate. I am the desperate one in the balcony. Look up. Here I am in the cheap section. Find me. I am not searching for enlightenment. I want peace."

He never looked up or gave any indication that he felt my presence, but he must have sensed I was there as my signals were intense. Maybe he was right to ignore my pleas.

Perhaps resolving my own problems was about to be my greatest lesson.

NASCA

We went out of Lima as often as we could during the winter, and spent the weekends in Nasca with Quique where it was dry and sunny. Nicky was friends with some of the local children, who went everywhere in groups; the older ones were in charge of the smaller ones and, even with the huge differences in age, they played together. When the children went swimming in the reservoir I kept an eye on them, otherwise they were on their own. They were a blur of motion, diving and swimming up and under like fish. I thought, "Why not put their energy to good use, and let them earn some money?"

I told Nicky: "I will pay you all to clear out the leaves floating on the surface of the reservoir." Even the youngest child, who couldn't swim, stood on the edge of the steps and helped by taking out everything he could safely reach. The job was quickly finished, and I handed Nicky the money to be divided between them.

They left straight away for the local shop, which was down a rocky unpaved road. The children went there by themselves, so I knew it was safe, but before they reached the shop a cab drove by and dropped someone at the hotel. Nicky stopped the cab on the way back, and negotiated a good price to take them into the centre of Nasca, where he thought they would find a larger selection of sweets for their money.

I was horrified when Quique told me where Nicky had taken his friends. Not all the children had followed him, some had run home and told their families where Nicky had taken the others. Fortunately, information moves slowly in Nasca, so by the time one of the parents told Quique and he remembered to tell me, the children were already safely home.

Everyone knew Nicky had instigated the trip, as nothing like that had ever happened there before. I went to find Nicky and took him back to our room. I asked him, "Nicky, what on earth were you thinking? Why did you go to Nasca? You can't take a cab there by yourself, it isn't safe."

He told me, "Mummy, I wasn't by myself, I was with my friends."

I said, "You aren't allowed to take a cab without an adult, and never without my permission. I didn't know where you were; if you were in danger I couldn't have protected you. Your friends aren't able to look after you, they're too young. That was a crazy thing to do."

He said: "No one told me I wasn't allowed to take a cab and you kept telling me you didn't worry about me here because Nasca was safe."

"Sweetheart, I might have said that it's safe at the hotel because we are isolated and everyone knows you, but I never told you that the city was safe. I don't know, maybe it is, but you are too young to judge for yourself, and you are too young to be there on your own."

He certainly seemed to be sincere, and I was sure we had never told him not to take a cab. It had never crossed my mind that I needed to. Nicky and I continued talking, and for the next hour I listed everything that I could possibly think of to tell him not to do.

MANCORA

W e were invited to spend a week in Mancora with friends whose house was just steps from the Pacific Ocean. I was also excited because they had asked me along for the drive. It was a long trip, twelve to thirteen hours, heading North on the Pan-American Highway, stopping just short of Ecuador. I didn't own a car, and because of the great distances in Peru Nicky and I usually flew to our destination. Mancora is a small coastal town, known for its miles of beaches and year-round surfing, very fashionable yet informal. It's within walking distance of Cabo Blanco, where Hemingway once fished for giant black marlin, and where they filmed "The Old Man and the Sea".

Quique dropped in to see us the night before we left. He wanted to say hello to Peter, who had just arrived from London, and to wish us a bon voyage. He stayed long enough for a drink and as he stepped into the lift to leave he remembered to tell me: "Watch out for the stingrays."

We set off before daybreak to avoid rush hour and arrive in Mancora before dark. John warned me that he wasn't going to stop except to refuel and to go to the loo, which suited me because I could see more of the country in the daylight. We talked the entire trip. Everyone I knew in Lima spoke English, but it was the English humour and the irony which could only be expressed by someone who knew more than just the mechanics of a language that I missed. Plus we had friends in common, and it was fun to reminisce. I had lived most of my adult life in London. I had friends there who I had known for more than thirty years and hearing their stories reminded me how much I missed it.

We arrived in Mancora earlier than expected. The caretaker came out to unload the car and he told me: "Señor Peter has just taken Nicky to one of the hotels for an early supper." I ran in their direction and found them at the first hotel. They had started their appetizer and it was too late to cancel the main course, so Peter asked the waiter to wrap up the food and we took it to the house with us.

Their dining room was separate from the house, facing the Pacific Ocean. It was rustic and unobtrusive, with a palm frond roof and open on the sides to let the breeze through, like a chickee hut. After dinner, we sat on the terrace and talked until early in the morning, with Nicky curled up asleep next to us. I mentioned Quique's warning about the stingrays, but everyone laughed. They told me: "We have been coming to Mancora for years and have never heard such absolute rubbish."

I had grown up in Florida with stingrays and said, "All you have to do is shuffle your feet going into the water. Stingrays will get out of your way if they know you are coming." I even demonstrated the shuffling technique while getting another drink, but no one was remotely interested.

Mancora reminded me of my childhood in Florida, and of my grandfather's property on the beach. At that time the houses around him were small and understated, and everyone knew their neighbours. Mancora didn't have the same fine white sandy beaches and the water was cold, but I enjoyed the simplicity and feeling of peace and isolation. After breakfast Nicky and I lounged around in hammocks, watching the fishermen drifting by on balsa rafts while Peter checked emails on the computer.

Vendors walked down the beach selling souvenirs. For years John had managed to keep them away, but Nicky quickly put an end to that. He loved looking at everything for sale and he would call them over to see if they had anything new. Nicky bought everything that he could talk his father into paying for, which was considerable. He bought shells, a shark's jaw filled with razor like teeth, wind chimes, dried seahorses, key chains and necklaces. Before long Nicky got a reputation for buying, so sellers would arrive early trying to tempt him into buying something new. At the same time some of the local dogs starting turning up because he fed them. Within days of our arrival, our cottage had become a mecca for sellers and strays. They arrived in droves, and at the end of the day they called out to Nicky and waved goodbye as they were heading home.

Everyone swam except me; the water was too cold. Instead I took walks or stayed at the cottage and read. One morning I watched as Peter carried Nicky back to the beach after swimming. Nicky didn't like walking through the maze of boulders, some taller than him, scattered just outside the shore. He was still small, and light enough to be swept off his feet and thrown against them by the waves. As they waded in, I saw Peter stumble. It looked as if he had tripped, almost falling with Nicky, but he recovered and carried Nicky the rest of the way to the beach. I went over to see what had happened, and when Nicky saw me he came running shouting: "Papi has been bitten by a jelly fish."

I laughed, thinking it was one of Nicky's jokes until I saw Peter staggering up the beach. He said, "No, it wasn't a jellyfish. I stepped on a bloody stingray."

I told him: "You've got to see a doctor."

He said, "Leave me alone. I'm in agony. I'm not going any-where." When Nicky was out of hearing range, he said, "I feel like a wounded bear, so keep out of my way." His foot was discoloured, it was beginning to swell and I knew it would get worse.

I told Nicky: "Come on, let's find John and see if he can talk some sense into your father. He's got to get the barb taken out and the sooner it comes out the better. If Papi refuses to go to the hospital, maybe you can ask the caretaker if he knows of a doctor who would come to us."

While we were looking for John one of the builders working on the kitchen came out. He had seen Peter limping up the beach, and asked us what happened. The man weighed about three hundred pounds and looked like a sumo wrestler. Nicky told him, "Papi stepped on a stingray." I added in broken Spanish, "He wasn't going to get help because he didn't believe me how serious it was."

The builder told us: "Don't worry, I know what to do."

Nicky and I hid behind the hedge and showed him where Peter was sitting. We stayed out of sight and watched while the builder went over and said a few words to Peter. Then he took Peter's foot, examined it for a moment, and started squeezing the barb out.

Peter was all but screaming and turning violet from the pain, but he wasn't going to argue with the builder, who had locked his leg in a vice-like grip and was determined to get the barb out. Peru is a macho society so it wasn't good form for Peter to beg the man to stop; and besides, he wasn't strong enough to make him stop. There was no escape.

After seeing the look on Peter's face, I thought it best to remain out of sight, so I took Nicky to my room to shower off the salt water and to get him into some dry clothes. After all, there wasn't anything we could do to help, and Peter had been given the option of going to a doctor who, I assumed would have given him a pain-killer before he removed the barb.

The next time we dared to look, the builder had Peter's foot in his mouth, and he was sucking between his toes. I thought, "Oh my God, this is too much. If only Peter were famous I could have taken a photo and sold it to the press and made my fortune." It was the kind of photo opportunity you could have waited a lifetime to get. It looked as if he was taking toe sucking to a new extreme, or that he was performing some other bizarre sexual act that living in the innocent environment of Peru we hadn't even heard of yet.

The builder proudly stuck out his tongue with part of the stingray's barb sitting on the end. Peter looked as if he had just given birth. He was sweating and pale as he politely thanked the builder, who was helping him back to his feet. Peter hobbled back to his room, peeled off his wet bathing suit, dropped it on the floor, and fell on the bed in agony.

I wanted to give Peter a little more time alone and a chance to recover, so Nicky and I went looking for John again. I was hoping that he might be able to convince Peter to go to the clinic. Peter needed to see a doctor, if for no other reason than to get an antibiotic and something for the pain. Their caretaker didn't know of a doctor who would come to us, and there wasn't a hospital in Mancora. There was only a small clinic near one of the petrol stations, and if it wasn't busy sometimes they closed early. If Peter did have problems later that night, we would have to drive to another town to find a clinic or a hospital that was open.

John came in and talked to Peter, and Peter immediately agreed to see a doctor. He was doubled over in pain, and seemed willing to try anything which might help. Peter was naked under the sheet so I brought over some clothes and started to help him get dressed. I gently swung his legs off the side of the bed and helped him to his feet, but when I was on my knees pulling up his shorts I got an irrepressible urge to tease, and speaking in the soft throaty voice of a seductress I told him: "I have an idea that might take your mind off your foot."

He looked daggers at me and said, "Muffi, I don't find your humour in the least bit funny."

Nicky who was sitting just outside the window listening, shot in and said, "Mummy, what did you say that wasn't funny?"

When we arrived at the clinic we were taken to a consulting room. There were none of the usual forms to fill out, no questions were asked, and when they had finished sweeping the sand out of the room Peter was put on a stainless steel table that resembled something normally used for post-mortems or by a veterinarian. It was reminiscent of the clinic that he took me to in the centre of Lima, but more primitive. I must say, it was in the back of my mind that if I had ever wanted to get even with Peter for taking me there, this was about as good as it got.

The woman who brought us to the room started to clean his wound with such ferocity that I couldn't bear to look, nor could John. It was verging on the inhumane. We were both sucking air in through our teeth and secretly thinking how happy we were that we weren't on that table. I don't think gentle or bedside manners were words often used around there, nor were rubber gloves or clean white uniforms. They must have been optional along with shoes; they were nowhere to be seen. It didn't look like she was going to waste any painkillers on Peter either. That was probably saved for the more serious cases like amputations.

After she had finished scouring his wound we were taken to another room. Peter, who is fastidious to a fault, limped barefoot across the filthy floor, keeping close behind us for protection. As we entered the room she told him he was going to be given an injection, which was painful and had to be injected in his gluteus maximus, i.e. the muscle of his bum. The nurse unlocked a small metal cabinet on the wall, and when she found a syringe large enough to accommodate all the vials she felt were absolutely necessary to his recovery, she set it aside, wrote down the names of the vials and took us to another room to pay before she was allowed to inject them. Peter gave us one last pitiful look, dropped his shorts and waited for the inevitable. We turned and looked the other way to give him some privacy, and as we did so found that we were face to face with a shiny, graphic illustration of a vagina, which dominated that side of the room.

I got the impression we were in the prenatal part of the clinic because of the vagina, and also because Peter was bent over steadying himself with one of the metal stirrups that they normally rest a woman's legs on when she is giving birth or having a gynaecological examination. John's young caretaker, who had accompanied us, gasped when he saw the huge glistening vagina, and he quickly swung back around, this time facing Peter's bum. He didn't know which way to look, and John and I, who were now facing him and the vagina, burst into hysterics after realizing his dilemma.

When the treatment was over the nurse gave Peter a painkiller, which knocked him out until late the next day.

CUSCO

C usco and Machu Picchu are at the top of everyone's 'to do' list when they visit Peru. Peter and I had talked about going there for years, but when we first came to Peru Nicky was so young that we were afraid he would suffer from the altitude, and we didn't want to leave him behind in Lima with friends. We agreed to set the trip aside until he was older, but somehow time flew by and we never went. Our plans of travelling to Cusco had long since been passed over for other places, but when Britt came to visit from London he wanted to see Machu Picchu, and he persuaded us, now that Nicky was old enough, that we should go there together.

We flew from sea level in Lima to Cusco, which is over eleven thousand feet. I took all of the usual precautions for altitude sickness – known locally as "soroche". We rested when we arrived at the hotel, and afterwards we sat outside in the courtyard and ate a light lunch. I drank endless cups of mate de coca, a remedy used for thousands of years and served to you upon arrival to protect against altitude sickness. Coca leafs are chewed, or served like tea, the same leaves as in cocaine but without the high.

Our hotel was once a monastery, built in the 16th century on the site of the palace of Inca Amaru Qhala. It is now a five star hotel owned by a European group and has every conceivable comfort, including oxygen pumped into some of the bedrooms. Wealthy tourists came in and out all day, which made the entrance of the hotel a desirable rendezvous for peddlers. One seller caught Nicky's attention by waving a thick stack of Intis, the old and defunct Peruvian currency, in his face. He told Nicky: "Here, quick, take them on credit. Don't worry. Your parents will pay."

Nicky and I wove our way out through the crowd, trying to make our escape, only to be caught by the beady eye of an old Cusquenian woman who, after we had broken away from the herd, had singled us out as easy prey. She was extravagantly dressed in traditional Andean costume and was trailing a well-groomed, fully decorated llama.

When she saw us alone she rushed forward, grabbing Nicky from me, insisting that such a beautiful child should be photographed next to her and her llama, but I pulled him back fearing the llama might kick him or bite. We tried to escape and hurried down to the Plaza de Armas, but she wasn't about to let us get away without a photo, and she followed us in hot pursuit with her llama's hooves clickety-clacking close behind us as we made our way down the ancient steps. I finally consented to the photo just to get rid of her, but the second I pressed the shutter she cornered me against the wall with the llama, its hot malodorous breath against my face, demanding twenty dollars for taking the photo.

Nicky laughed when he saw my predicament. He knew my phobia of large hoofed animals with teeth, and after my desperate tug of war to save him from the llama he found it hilarious to see me cornered with the llama in my face. Though terrified, I stood my ground and argued vehemently over the price. I wasn't about to give into her exorbitant fee. Furthermore I was incensed to be mistaken for a common tourist, and I bargained around her llama's head in a Spanish that she could make no sense of. She looked relieved when Nicky came to my rescue. She gladly accepted the money he offered and pulled the llama away.

We walked along the Inca wall and found the twelve angle stone, its complicated multiform shape fitting into the surrounding stones like the finishing piece in a jigsaw puzzle. Afterwards we walked around the Plaza de Armas and visited the Cathedral of Santo Domingo, also known as Cusco Cathedral, which was built on the site of Viracocha's palace. Inside there is an overwhelming amount of woodwork, religious artefacts, ornate silver and gold, all crafted by local artists, and an important collection of paintings from the Cusquenian School. The painting most commonly pointed out to tourists and shown in all the guidebooks is the primitive representation of Jesus and the Apostles seated at the Last Supper. Stretched out on a platter in front of Jesus is the unmistakable body of a roasted guinea pig.

I felt nauseous and light-headed from the altitude, but I kept going because I didn't want to miss out on anything. By the time we returned to the hotel, I felt too ill to eat and wanted to sleep; we had an early start in the morning to catch the train. Nicky and I stayed in our room, and I collapsed on the bed, hoping that Nicky would do the same while Peter joined Britt for supper. But as soon as Peter left, Nicky complained that he was hungry too and he wanted me to order him something to eat. With a pounding head, I dragged myself across the room to find a menu and to ring room service. When Nicky's dinner arrived, I signed the bill and watched while the waiter ceremoniously lifted the heavy silver lid, but the smell of food made me sick and I only just made it back to the bathroom before throwing up again.

I hoped that after some sleep I would feel better, but in the morning I felt worse. The throbbing in my head was unbearable. It hurt to move my eyes. Every molecule of my body was screaming out in pain. I couldn't believe my body would let me down so badly, and that just as I was on the verge of seeing Machu Picchu I could barely get out of bed. There was nothing else I could do except bury my face in my pillow and cry, out of pain and frustration.

Peter sent for the doctor, who came straight away with pills and an assistant lugging a bottle of oxygen. Swallowing the pills made me ill, and I staggered back to the bathroom and started vomiting again. Altitude sickness is insidious. It can strike at any time, on arrival or days later. It has nothing to do with fitness or age, and it affects everyone differently. Sleeplessness, headaches, or nausea are all common, but at times a person can become so debilitated that they have to be brought down to a lower altitude in order to recover.

There was no choice. Peter and Nicky had to leave without me in order to catch the train. Our tickets had been booked weeks in advance in order to get seats. It would have been impossible to change all the tickets for the following day. We had no way of knowing when I would feel better. Peter and Nicky begged me to come, but I felt too ill to get up. Peter even offered to carry me to the train. He told me: "Get up you'll feel better if you go. Machu Picchu is more than three thousand feet lower than Cusco." But I didn't have the strength to get dressed. I watched them leave and then somehow, I fell into a deep sleep. It must have been about an hour later when I was awoken by the phone. It was Peter ringing me from the train. "Muffi, are you alright? We're on the train. Are you feeling any better?" As I was talking to him, I realized I no longer had a headache. I told him: "Yes, my headache has gone. I must have fallen asleep. Thanks for ringing. Give Nicky and Britt my love."

After putting down the phone, I started to go back to bed, and then I realized that if I slept now, tomorrow I would have to go to Machu Picchu by myself, and I didn't want to go there alone. I rang the front desk and told them: "I have to get to Machu Picchu."

Someone at reception told me: "I am sorry, but the trains for Machu Picchu have already left."

I beseeched him for help. I told him: "Please, there has to be a way. There is always a way." I asked for any suggestions, even those with the remotest possibilities, and I persisted until he told me: "It might be possible for you to catch the train at the first station. Up until then there is a series of switchbacks, which slow the train down to a snail's pace. I will order you a car, but don't get your hopes up, it's very late."

I thanked him for his help, and said, "I will be out front as soon as I can get there." As I was sucking oxygen and getting dressed I thought back to the time when I would have happily stayed behind at a five star hotel, spoiling myself and ringing room service. I would have enjoyed going to Machu Picchu alone. I had always travelled by myself, because of the freedom. But Peter and I had talked about going to Machu Picchu for so many years, and going there together with Nicky, that I suddenly felt very left out and alone. I also realized that I was no longer used to freedom or doing anything on my own.

When I finished dressing, I took my last breath of oxygen from the tank, filling my lungs to bursting point. I rushed through the lobby and found my cab waiting outside the front door. Time was of the essence. I jumped in the cab and off we went. After the initial rush of getting out of town, the driver noticed I wasn't looking well. When he recognised an herb by the side of the road that he thought would help with altitude sickness, he stopped to pick it for me. He hadn't told me what he was doing, or perhaps he had tried to do so, but in his enthusiasm for finding the plant his Spanish had become too fast for me to follow. All I knew was that he had stopped on a dangerous curve and we were almost killed by a bus coming around the bend.

I was terrified but it didn't faze him in the slightest. He just waved to the driver and everyone he knew on the bus and, afterwards, to everyone on the next bus that managed to avoid the first bus and us. When he thought it looked safe, he jumped out of the car and dashed across the road, leaving me in the car while he picked the plant. At first it seemed as if the altitude and lack of oxygen might have affected his reasoning. I had no idea what he was doing, and when he ran back to the car waving a plant he had ripped out by the roots I panicked and didn't know whether to lock all the doors or to run.

He rubbed the herb between his hands until it turned into a fine liquid. Then he smeared the green mess under my nose and told me to breathe it in. When he finished he jumped back in the car and started driving again. A little further down the road he tossed me a bag of dried coca leaves and told me to eat some, and to keep breathing in the herbs. With my now greener than ever face, I sat in the back chewing coca leaves. I was no longer concerned with catching the train. I had fulfilled my need for adventure and would have been happy to drive around a bit longer and then go back to bed. This had been enough excitement for one day.

His cellular phone rang and broke my reverie. To my astonishment he handed me his phone. It was the hotel ringing to say: "I'm sorry, but you left the hotel so quickly we didn't have a chance to give you your ticket. We are faxing the station to say you are on your way and, hopefully, the stationmaster will allow you on the train without one."

We were flying around the mountain curbs. I was chewing coca leaves and humming Peruvian songs mingled with "She'll be coming round the mountain when she comes." I had developed a keen taste for the coca leaves and had eaten more than he had suggested. I hadn't eaten breakfast or dinner for that matter, and the coca leaves had a nice sort of dry, crunchy breakfast cereal sort of taste. The drive was magical, and I travelled along enjoying the view until he suddenly jolted me back to reality by honking the horn and shouting: "Señora, el tren!"

And there it was, just next to us. We were parallel with the train. My driver was honking his horn like a maniac. He told me: "I am signalling the driver we are coming, but we will still need a lot of luck to catch it at the station. They have a schedule to keep. He won't be able to wait."

The train was on a straight line, whereas our road wasn't. We were racing around curves and going through villages that were out of history books. The atmosphere was now tense. I had to catch the train. I started spitting on my hands and rubbing some of the green slime off my face while trying to get my things together. Then, in what seemed like no time at all, we screeched to a halt in front of a small station and he told me: "Get out and run to the train."

When I got to the gate it was already padlocked shut. I collapsed against the cool metal bars and thought to myself, I had gotten so close, I was only going to miss the train by seconds, and now I would have to watch as they pulled away from the station without me. My eyes were filling up, getting ready to overflow and embarrass me at any moment.

There could be no consolation for missing the train, which I could almost reach through the bars and touch. A wave of nausea and disappointment enveloped me as I watched the train jerk forward and slowly start to pull away. My face was pressed between the metal bars when the stationmaster saw me, ran over and asked my name. He seemed to know who I was and fumbled with his keys to open the gate. Then he blew his whistle and stopped the train.

When I reached their carriage, Nicky was looking out of the window, and he shouted: "Mummy!"

Peter didn't turn around. He thought Nicky was being silly and continued talking to Britt. So when I appeared in front of them and said a rather loud "Hello" for effect, he jumped. My grandmother would have loved the moment. She was forever telling me, "Never underestimate the power of a grand entrance," and from the looks on their faces it was easy to appreciate that she was right. My arrival there would be long remembered. I wondered when such an opportunity would ever present itself again.

As the train began to move I looked out of the window. The taxi driver was still there, standing with the stationmaster, and when he saw me he began jumping up and down on the platform, waving goodbye as if we were dear old friends. He wasn't in a hurry to get back to work, having just earned enough money to retire for the day. There had been no time to negotiate the price, and he swore on some local saint that he had no change as I was his first customer that day. So I had handed him my only bill, feeling a combination of gratitude and exasperation.

Once I had caught my breath, Nicky and I went back and stood in the aisle while I told Peter and Britt all about my adventure to find them. Peter told me they had heard us honking and saw someone waving, but he hadn't realized who it was. He thought it was an overzealous train fanatic or a lunatic. Peter, like me, tends to exaggerate about illnesses and almost everything. I imagined that Britt would have been less surprised if someone had come aboard to break the news of my demise rather than see me step onto the train.

The next day we took a bus tour to Sacsayhuaman, an ancient walled Inca complex on the outskirts of Cusco. Our bus headed north, climbing higher, and in a short time we arrived at Sacsayhuaman, one of the most interesting archaeological sites in Peru. As soon as Nicky stepped off the bus he saw a group of people on top of a hill which overlooked the ruins. He begged: "Mummy, may I go up and see where they're looking?"

I didn't have the stamina to take him, but the guide assured me it was safe and that Nicky could go on his own and easily catch up. I told him: "Yes go, but hurry, I'll wait." I walked along with the guide who was telling us about the construction of Sacsayhuaman. She said it was supposed to be built in the 1500s, but when it was written about in the mid-1500s by Garcilaso de la Vega, the bastard son of a Spaniard who was raised there, no one interviewed by him remembered anything about its construction. She said: "Sacsayhuaman was estimated to have taken seventy years to build, using a workforce of more than twenty thousand men. So if the dates were true and it was finished in the early fifteen hundreds, it seems impossible that everyone involved in its construction, and their families, would have disappeared by the time he wrote about it."

She told us the massive stones were hauled from a quarry that was miles away. The technology needed to cut and move such enormous stones, and the construction of Sacsayhuaman, was so advanced that the Spanish wouldn't accept that Indians who had no written language, and who they described as another animal species, were capable of accomplishing such an extraordinary feat. The heaviest stone, weighing well over a hundred tons, fits so precisely together with the surrounding stones without the use of mortar that a blade of grass couldn't be slipped between them. They attributed the work to a higher power or enchantment. Even today, with modern technology and equipment, Sacsayhuaman would be difficult, if not impossible, to replicate.

Nicky made it to the top of the hill just as our group was entering a cave. He shouted: "Mummy!" I turned around to wave and waited outside for him. He shouted: "Mummy!" again, but this time he was running down the hill instead of using the steps. He slipped and started sliding down a steep slope. Somehow, he managed to get back on his feet and continued running down the hill, gaining momentum. What he couldn't see was that the next part of the slope dropped off and went straight down to the rocks below.

I ran toward him screaming: "Nicky, stop! Stop! Don't move, stay still!"

Some of the guards saw what was happening and they ran with me. I climbed over a wall and tried to climb up to reach him, but he was too far away. One of the guards ran past me, I couldn't keep up, so I collapsed against the mountain and prayed. My mind went into another dimension, where I could no longer think or feel. I was only aware of my breathing, and the sound of blood pulsing through my ears. Nicky was somewhere above me, and I held the vision of him running down the slope calling, "Mummy." Then I saw the guard with Nicky under his arm climbing down to meet me. Several guards were around me, calming me, as they helped me down from the ledge.

It was impossible to disconnect from my present state and to feel what was happening in the present. In my mind it looked as if he were running to his death. I couldn't dare come back to the present until I convinced myself that this child I was holding was real and not an illusion, and that he wasn't just my mind playing some perverse trick to preserve my sanity. Nicky kept talking to me. I could hear him, but his voice seemed surreal. He was covered in dust. I picked bits of earth from his hair and continued examining him, afraid that at any moment he might disappear.

I don't know how Nicky had managed to stop sliding, or how the guard was able to carry him down from the ledge. Nicky was almost the same height as the guard, but he carried him down as if he weighed nothing. After brushing some dirt off his clothes, I buried my face in his hair, breathing in his essence. It was such a great relief to hold him. As if through some miracle, I was given a second chance to appreciate there was no greater gift in my life than this child. Somehow the shock cleared something so deep that everything in my heart surfaced at once, allowing me to see how my very existence and happiness had become inseparable from him. There he was in my arms, smiling and asking: "Mummy, are you okay? Are those real tears? Mummy, are you really crying? Would you have been really angry with me if I had died just then?" "Mummy, can we just start again and pretend that this never really happened. Okay? Will I still get a prize for good behaviour? Can

I have one last chance? Okay, Mummy? Please. Come on Mummy; give me one of your happy faces, just a little smile to show me you're not upset. Okay?"

After I pulled myself together and found the strength to walk I thanked the guards again and again. I didn't know how to stop thanking them. At that moment I wasn't confident enough with my Spanish to trust saying anything else. I had wanted to say so much more, but I could see that even without words they understood.

When I couldn't thank them one more time without sounding ridiculous, I put on my hat and sunglasses. We smiled at each other and Nicky and I left to re-join the group. We found them deep inside the cave, huddled together in front of a stone altar, silently listening to the guide telling us that it had once been used to sacrifice children. I felt strange being there holding Nicky's hand and searched the air for a clue as to how the families must have felt, watching the life blood of their precious children draining away to please the gods in the ultimate sacrifice. Perhaps their spirits still inhabited the place and they had been the ones who spared Nicky and me from a similar fate. We stood in awe looking at the massive altar, feeling ill at ease in its presence.

Then, hand in hand, we followed our group back to the bus.

BULLFIGHT IN LIMA

Salvador rang early on Sunday morning and invited me to a bullfight. He said: "Gringa, this is the last fight of the season. It's your last chance to go. Come on, say yes, and I will pick you up at noon."

At first, I thought he was joking, but when I realized he wasn't I said no. My family had once taken me to a bullfight in Portugal when I was young, and I had suffered through every moment of the fight. But Salvador wouldn't accept no for an answer. He kept badgering me until he wore me down and somehow convinced me that, after living in Lima for so many years, it was verging on the unpatriotic to shun bullfighting.

He asked: "Muffi, how can you claim to love Peru with such undying affection when you reject one or our most beloved traditions?"

His last minute invitation worried me. It suggested desperation, free tickets, or that he couldn't find anyone else who would go with him. It was against my better judgement that I agreed to accompany him.

We took a taxi through the centre of Lima to get there, past the railroad tracks, past everything familiar, and at the end of the street we saw the Plaza de Toros, standing in all its splendour. As we approached the long line of traffic at the main intersection, Salvador decided that it would be faster to walk the short distance remaining. He paid the driver and told me: "Quick, jump out of the cab before the light changes".

I was grateful to see that there was a tiny island where we could stand to protect us from the cars and trucks that were now whizzing past us in all directions. But, after glancing down and seeing its crumbling curbs from the countless times it had already been run over, I no longer felt that lucky. Peruvians pride themselves on their driving skills when manoeuvring their cars, motorcycles or even carts and busses in and out of traffic at breakneck speed. Pedestrians crossing the street are seen as an impediment, to be frightened out of the way. I found it ironic that we were probably in more danger of being killed just crossing the road to get there than the matador was ever going to be during the bullfight.

As we entered the Plaza, Salvador pointed out a small plaque explaining that the ring was several hundred years old. He told me: "It was built before the independence of the United States." I imagined how, for hundreds of years, Salvador's family came to this arena, watching the bullfights, socializing, and enjoying themselves; while my ancestors were building log cabins or planting corn and probably not having much fun.

Hundreds of people were milling around inside the Plaza and every other person we met was a friend or a cousin of Salvador. I have been told that there are only two things in Peru that start on time: the bullfights and the cinema. So, after greeting his family and friends, we quickly went inside and found our seats. Salvador pointed to the shadow falling on our side of the arena and told me: "Look we have good seats. We are on the shady side, they cost double than those in the sun."

I responded: "Look, some of the seats in the front row also have shade. Why aren't we sitting there?"

He said: "Those seats were reserved for the aficionados who buy their seats for the season. The privilege of obtaining those seats is sometimes passed from father to son. That row is called the barrera. The second row is called contrabarrera. They are the only rows with names. The rest of the rows in the arena, like ours, have numbers."

I told him: "Salva, I've got a name for our seats."

He asked: "Okay what is it?"

I said: "Our row should be called the barriada," which is the name of a shantytown or a slum.

He told me: "Very funny. Next time bring a hat."

The bullfight began as the matadors came out to the wild applause of the audience. They were all foreign: two from Spain, and one from the south of France. I asked Salvador: "Where are all the Peruvian matadors?" but he didn't respond. I commiserated with him. I told him: "In a city of millions, that's known for having the oldest bullfighting arena in the Americas, it seems odd you couldn't have come up with a matador. No wonder you want to drop the subject."

Shortly after the introduction, the first bull charged into the ring and the music stopped abruptly. The matador twirled his cape in the traditional manner and the bull made several passes at him, but it seemed far more intent on attacking the wooden barriers than in attacking the matador. I started to relax and thought for a moment that I might enjoy bullfighting after all. It was an ancient sport, an art as Salvador insisted. It was a pleasure being there and sitting outside surrounded by hundreds of cheering aficionados on a beautiful day. The atmosphere in the arena was of an enormous fiesta. So far everything was perfect. I loved the crowds and the excitement. This was a part of Peru that I had allowed myself to miss. I had refused, for years, to come to a bullfight and all because of a bad experience I had suffered when I was young.

My mind swept back to Portugal and to my first bullfight. My father had promised me the bull wouldn't be killed, otherwise I wouldn't have gone. As they stabbed it with the first banderillas, I wanted to run away. I begged my father to let me leave, but he told me: "No, it's too dangerous for you to go on your own. You might not recognize our driver and get lost." There were huge crowds and beggars outside the entrance gate. "Just close your eyes," he insisted, "it will soon be over." The woman sitting directly in front of us looked at home and sat posture perfect on the hard bench. She wore a tailored suit and a jaunty hat perched on one side of her head. She was young and elegant. She was also sympathetic and turned to me from time to time, patting my knee, talking softly and telling me not to cry, reassuring me: "Don't worry, they won't kill the bull until after it leaves the ring." I was shocked when she told me. I stammered back: "They kill the bull, even if it won?" She said: "Yes, once it is injured and in pain, it will be even more dangerous. It will hate all men." When my father wasn't listening, I whispered back: "You can hardly blame it." After realizing that I had been more or less deceived about the fate of the bull, I cried with impunity. I felt my father's shame that I hadn't mastered my emotions and that I could cry with such childish abandon in public. Sentiment was a fine emotion, but not where bulls were concerned; and not when it drew attention to the fact that I thought the fight and their culture of bullfighting was an abomination.

My mind shot back to the present as the picadors trotted in on their padded horses. No sooner had the bull crossed the ring than one of the picadors moved in and stabbed a lance deep between its shoulder blades, viciously breaking open its tough hide. I gagged as Salvador filled me in on the gory details telling me, "They needed to cut the muscles to keep its head low." When he saw the expression on my face he said: "What? It's nothing." Then he held out his hand to demonstrate, saying: "Look the point of the lance is no longer than the width of my hand and there is a thick band to prevent it from going deeper."

At first I thought I would be sick. I swallowed back bile and asked him: "What are you talking about? Why would they need more than a four-inch blade to cripple it? The muscle and bones are just below the surface of the skin."

The bull let out a startled cry and then looked directly at the man who, for no apparent reason, had just inflicted so much pain on him. I broke out into a cold sweat as another wave of nausea washed over me, but there was no easy escape. I was now trapped in my seat by hundreds of legs, so I considered my options and decided that it would be better to stay put with Salvador, rather than to try and leave and risk getting sick on the feet or the lap of someone I didn't know. In desperation, I summoned a waiter to bring me a beer, and with my sweaty shaking hand I drank it down in one go. Afterwards Salvador got into an argument with the waiter who refused to give me back the correct change. He remained standing in front of us, blocking everyone's view, hoping that we would shoo him away and not worry about the money, but unlike most people, Salvador wasn't intimidated and kept threatening the vendor until he gave in and handed him the change. When I tried to buy another beer from the man, Salvador was incensed. He told me: "No. I would rather curse a friend than let you buy another thing from that thief!"

The bull stood motionless until the matador got fed up and threw his hat at its head. That revived the audience's attention. He seemed more aggressive than the bull. After being taunted and provoked, the bull charged again and as it charged it was stabbed with the barbed darts called banderillas. Salvador told me: "They are used to liven it up." I said: "Are you crazy, the bull is in agony. Look the dart is stuck in his muscle, every time he moves it tears him apart, the pain must be excruciating. The bull is fighting for his life against that sadist."

This fight was going nowhere, so instead of swinging the cape in front of him or holding it off to his side, the matador swung his cape behind him and motioned the bull forward by humping the air with his hips. He appeared to be trying to provoke the bull into charging directly at him. I asked Salvador: "Has the man lost his mind. Does he want to be castrated?" After the picadors had cut its muscles, the bull could barely lift his head so the man's crotch was about as high as he could reach. The matador continued thrusting his pelvis towards the bull, which was facing in our direction, causing us to become involuntarily transfixed on his, dare I say, unusually prominent groin, instead of on the motionless bull. I nudged Salvador and said: "Wow, it looks like the Spanish are better endowed than Peruvian men. Is it real?" But Salvador pretended he wasn't listening.

I wanted to understand bullfighting. I began bombarding Salvador with questions and driving him crazy. I was amazed to learn that a good bullfighter could earn millions of dollars a year. That was reason enough to want to kill bulls. Matador literally means "killer." The crowd was crying for blood. They reminded me of a lynch mob, and I sank lower in my seat.

The next matador came out and teased the powerful bull, like in a childish game, seeming to say: "Come and get me." That is where the similarity ended. After he got enough attention from the bull, he killed it. But not with one thrust of the sword, which Salvador had promised me. He swore on some ancient saint that the bull would die instantly when the blade hit its heart; but it wasn't true. Or maybe the matador missed the heart, because the bull didn't die. The matador put the entire length of the blade of his sword inside the bull two or three times. Still he struggled to his feet, as if pleading for some gesture of humanity. Blood bubbled from his nose as he fell forward to his knees; too weak to escape, pitifully watching his tormentors closing in around him. I told Salvador: "If watching them torture an animal gives you pleasure, you should see a psychiatrist. This is sickening."

When the bull could no longer struggle to his feet someone inside the ring took pity on him and stabbed him in the brain with a dagger, swiftly ending his suffering. I said, "I never thought I would be grateful to see an animal stabbed in the head but, after this odious bullfight, it was a small relief." I told him: "You are deluding yourself. There is no sport in bull fighting. The bull is the loser, no matter how well he fights. It's not a contest when the odds are so obviously stacked against the opponent. The matador acts as your proxy. He is sent in and paid to do what you are afraid to do. Maybe it's the bull's masculinity that intimidates you. After a good fight, you castrate the bull and eat its balls to enhance your virility. Well, that has got to tell you something about the mentality of the people who like this 'sport'." I told him: "When you die, I hope you're reincarnated as a bull. I don't care that you are Catholic and don't believe in reincarnation. If there is any justice at all in this universe, and I believe there is, that should be your fate."

He said, "That's fine. I will have fun frolicking around the fields having my way with the cows, and it will only take a few minutes to die nobly in the ring."

I pointed to the ring to remind him: "Not if you get that matador."

I found the bullfighters strangely effeminate in the way they posed; their narrow hips thrust forward, taunting, confidently showing off their graceful figures, like models, and in the way they dressed. They behaved like seductive young girls, innocently teasing, trying to catch the attention of the bull, which would then, in turn, make advances toward them as if in some dangerous sexual game.

Salvador told me: "You are so obtuse. Everyone knows bullfighters are masculine."

I replied: "You are too brainwashed to be objective. I dare you to dress in the same tight ornate trousers of a matador and enter a bar in Lima while thrusting your hips at the men, pretending they are the bull. That way, we could get a more impartial opinion. I'm willing to bet you wouldn't make it out of there alive. You're not fast enough."

The next bull charged out and made up for all the previous bulls by attacking everything that moved. He was fearless and, while the picador was cutting his muscles, the bull continued charging into the heavily padded horse, which at the same moment allowed the picador more time to thrust the lance deep between his shoulder blades. When the picador withdrew his spear, the bull stood motionless in the ring except for a slight swaying. After a few minutes a rumour circulated around the audience that, "The bull has broken his leg."

I told Salvador: "That's rubbish. He's bleeding internally. He's dying! Look for yourself. The bull is going to keel over. He isn't limping. He can barely stand."

The bull waited quietly in the ring while the officials debated what to do next. The audience roared. This crowd was not going to be easily placated, and they continued shouting and stamping their feet in the rafters; making a terrible racket. They had come to watch a fight, not a slaughter. The audience was incensed.

There was no escape for the officials. They were now trapped in their seats by the angry crowd and were easily convinced not to make their decision based on economics. If they wanted to get out of the stadium in one piece, they had better come up with another bull, and they had better get this one out of the ring before it fell down dead. Suddenly, the heavy gates swung open and a small group of cows were herded in to befriend him. They surrounded the wounded bull as if to protect him; and then slowly, and pitifully, they left the ring together.

We were given a lift home by one of Salvador's cousins, who asked me what I thought of the bullfight. I told him: "I didn't like it," and in deference to Salvador I left it at that. His cousin told me: "Oh, Americans never like bullfights, they don't understand them." He insisted: "Ask me some questions, so you can better acquaint yourself with bullfighting. Maybe the next time you will enjoy it more."

Salvador cringed.

I said: "You haven't by chance read Freud? The fight seemed to me all about man's conflict between masculinity and vulnerability. I know nothing about bullfighting, but it looked as if the matador was addressing some dark psychological fear in men, maybe castration complex. By thrusting his groin at the bull, he was confronting his fear of castration." I could tell he hadn't read Freud and that he saw no merit in my interpretation so I asked: "Why are the picadors allowed to cut the muscles in the bull's neck?"

He said: "It is done for their own good. It keeps their head down, making it easier for a clean and more precise kill. That way the bull doesn't suffer. Plus, it's dangerous for the matador if they didn't cut the muscles."

I said: "I don't know any other sport in the world that allows you to physically handicap your opponent without automatic disqualification."

From the ensuing silence I knew our discussion had ended, and that I would almost certainly never be invited to another bullfight.

Which was fine with me.

OWL

I t was still dark when I was awoken by a loud thumping noise outside my bedroom. At first, I thought it was an earthquake, which shakes the windows and causes them to bang together against the frame, but I discovered that the sound was coming from a large owl beating its wings against the window as it struggled to keep from falling backwards off the narrow ledge. The owl was facing me, and as I sat up it flew to the balcony of the next room. I have always thought of owls as good luck, and I imagined that this owl was a messenger of better things to come.

In the morning, I rushed into the kitchen to tell Nicky about the owl. When he heard the word owl he stopped eating and stared at me incredulously. At first, I thought my story had aroused a curiosity in him. He told me: "Mummy, don't you know that if you look in the eyes of an owl at night someone in your family will be dead in the morning."

I was shocked by his comment. I am the one who is superstitious, Nicky isn't. I took a deep breath and told him: "Nicky that is total rubbish. Owls are good luck."

I repeated the story to Nancy, who was working in the kitchen, and asked her, "Aren't owls good luck?"

She looked nervous, not knowing what to say; afterwards she checked to make sure that I had only seen it from my bedroom window. After that she didn't speak. I asked her again, "Aren't owls good luck?" Since she declined to answer, I concluded by telling them: "People often keep small figures of owls for good luck."

She replied: "Señora Muffi, I hope so." Then she left for her day off as quickly as she could get out of the flat.

Later I asked Armandina: "Aren't owls good luck?" To which she replied: "No." So I asked Marina, Quique's maid, who worked part-time for us. She thought for a moment and said: "The last time I heard about someone seeing an owl…." then she hesitated, "I don't think you really want to know." Nevertheless, she proceeded to tell me in great detail of the misfortune that befell them. Fortunately, I didn't understand everything she was saying but, even with my limited Spanish, I knew "dying" and "cancer" featured prominently in her story.

Later I asked Quique about the owl. He wasn't much help either. He looked puzzled and asked: "Why do you think an owl would want to land outside your window?" He said he had never heard they were bad luck but, then again, he had never heard of an owl coming to someone's window before either, "Que raro!" – "How strange!"

When my friends arrived for lunch, someone asked: "Why do you keep touching the crucifix around your neck?"

I told them the story of the owl, and everyone laughed except Salvador. He thought for a moment and became serious as he began recounting a story from his youth. He told us: "Many years ago, I was staying at my brother-in-law's Hacienda with my family, and after dinner we returned to the drawing room and found a black moth on the wall. When my brother-in-law saw the moth, he became alarmed and told us that it was a sign, and that someone in the room would soon be dead. The next morning he went riding. No one knows why he crossed a torrential stream, but when he didn't return for breakfast they searched, and found that both he and the horse had been swept downstream to their deaths." Salvador concluded: "I have never heard anything about owls being bad luck, only moths."

When Nicky was getting ready for bed, owls popped back into the conversation. I asked him: "What about Harry Potter? Didn't some of the boys in the story have owls? Were they bad luck?" To which he replied: "Mummy, that's Hollywood ... this is real." Then Armandina came in and the owl conversation started up again in earnest. Except this time she began reciting a little rhyme about owls that her mother had taught her when she was a child.

I didn't understand one of the words and I asked Nicky what it meant, but he didn't know either. So he asked her, and she explained it meant hooting. That word seemed to jog something in her memory and she asked me: "Did it hoot?" I told her: "No, it just looked at me." She seemed genuinely relieved as she told me: "That's good. No one is supposed to die unless they heard it hoot."

Afterward, Nicky eyed me suspiciously and said: "Mummy, are you sure it didn't hoot?" I told him, "Not a peep."

I didn't have the heart to remind him that, after being married to his father, I still sleep with earplugs.

SECOND BULLFIGHT WITH SALVADOR

I was surprised when Salvador invited me to another bullfight. He added, "You can bring a friend," but, before I had a chance to say no, he enticed me by saying that he was one of the matadors and that after the fight we were invited to the owner's house for a fiesta.

I said, "I'll go to the party, but I don't want to watch you slaughter bulls."

He told me: "This is a Tienta, which is different from a bullfight; they use cows instead of bulls. It looks like a bullfight except the animals aren't hurt, it's bloodless. La Tienta is to demonstrate the bravery and ferocity of the female calves. Afterward, the most fearless and aggressive animals are selected and sold off for breeding, thereby maintaining a bloodline of strong ferocious bulls. For the calves fierce enough to be selected, theirs will be a life of sex and frolicking in the sun."

I said, "Alright, that sounds like fun."

The party wasn't far from Lima. We took the road south and drove for miles down one of the main roads until we found the wall of the estate. There we turned right and followed the boundary wall down a dirt road. The entrance was easy to spot; it was lined with employees who were waiting outside to direct us into a parking space. There weren't many guests, maybe forty, all of whom were old friends. For most of the people there this was an annual event, but for me it was new and exciting. We kissed everyone hello and were offered drinks and some canapés before being led across the lawn to a private bullring.

While we were waiting for the fight to begin, a troop of waiters circled around us flourishing trays of Pisco Sours, whisky, and Inca Kola. The matadors were a tight group of childhood friends, all of them fanatics about bullfighting. They wore street clothes, not matador costumes, which was good because most of them were well passed the days when they had the lithe supple figures normally associated with bullfighters.

When the fight was announced the first matador stepped boldly into the ring, twirled his cape and seemed surprisingly nonchalant considering the heavily scarred gates were swinging open and that, any second, a large horned animal would charge out, ready to attack anything that moved. The audience waited in rapt silence. I closed my eyes and braced myself for bloodshed and mutilation, wishing I hadn't come. Until a loud burst of laughter caused me to look up, and there, cowering near the gate was a tiny calf, who appeared too terrified to enter. The matador took ages to provoke it into charging and, with all of the effort of the charge, the calf, with its weak unstable legs, skidded to a halt in front of the matador and fell flat on its face. He looked down on it and with great tenderness took hold of its little horns and lifted it back to its feet. Afterward he bowed to the wild applause of the audience. In spite of her popularity, she wasn't going to be selected to strengthen the bloodline living out her days in sexual bliss; she was probably going to be amongst those chosen for to-night's supper.

Next to enter the ring was an adolescent calf with more spirit, and much larger than the previous one. The calf scraped a line deep in the ground with its hoof, clouding the air in dust. The matador held the cape taunt and lunged towards it on one foot with enough force to catch the calf's attention. It turned, and then charged the cape repeatedly until it was foaming at the mouth and panting heavily. When the matador felt he had spent enough time in the ring he bowed and with the final flourish of his cape he disappeared through one of the narrow exits.

The inside of the ring is surrounded by a wooden fence, called la barrera, which is broken by four shielded openings – los burlade-ros. Each opening is wide enough for a man to squeeze through and escape, but not a bull. However, as the matador was leaving, the calf charged again, and because it was so thin it easily slipped through the opening and followed him out of the ring. The mata-dor had a narrow lead as they circled along the passageway - el callejón - to where the rest of the matadors were awaiting their turn. There were roars of laughter from the crowd. The matador was only inches ahead of the calf. Chaos ensued as it raced down the passageway knocking the slower bullfighters out of its way. The waiters shot well into the lead with the drinks. Several people from the audience helped by reaching down and taking the heavy silver trays, then pulling the waiters up and over the wall to safety so that they could continue serving us drinks.

Everything was back under control. José the next matador en-tered the ring. This calf wasn't familiar with the rules. It didn't follow the cape, but instead charged forward, bit hold of José's arm and dragged him to the ground, covering him in long vis-cous strings of saliva. The following matador had worse luck, when he was scooped up between the heifer's horns and then slammed against the barrier, after having ridden there on her head. Shortly afterwards, another matador was knocked down by a calf, which then inadvertently tripped over his prostrate body and landed on top of him. I'm afraid she stepped on him in several places as she struggled to her feet. This time I felt sorry for the matadors. Clearly, the cows had won.

After the wounded matadors were cleaned and bandaged in loo paper and sanitary napkins, as these were all they could find for first aid, we were escorted to lunch. Our host arranged a live band for entertainment, and next to the dance floor there was an enormous buffet spread out across four or five tables. After the meal, I was invited by one of the matadors to dance. He was a brilliant dancer, and as he struggled to twirl me around the room he told me: "Gringa, loosen up." But I couldn't. Later he suggested: "You might want to consider a few dancing lessons while you are in living in Lima."

I am a dreadful dancer. I feel awkward and out of place on the dance floor. I stick out, especially in Peru where, even the most unassuming person can surprise you by dancing like a dream; it's in their blood. I've watched people stumble up to the dance floor but, once they catch the rhythm, they are transformed into other beings. Not me. I'm stiff and uncoordinated and I hate to be led. However at least I had the good manners not to suggest that he could equally benefit from a diet and some instruction before entering the bullring again. As the dance floor was filling up and the Pisco Sours coursed through my veins, I too became transformed, though perhaps only in my own mind.

I continued dancing without inhibition until my friends thought it wise to take me home.

HUANCAYO

During a trip to London I came across an advertisement stating that the passenger service from Lima to Huancayo Peru would be starting again. Due to terrorism in the 1990s, passenger service had been suspended, and the train was relegated to cargo only. The trip was advertised internationally as the highest passenger train ride in the world, which at the time it was, climbing up to 15,700 feet, just below the highest peak of Mont Blanc. It went through 66 tunnels, over 59 bridges, and took about 12 hours from the centre of Lima to get there. I ripped out the article and brought it back to Lima. Peter and I had seen parts of the railroad on the drive to Tarma. We watched the cargo trains skirting the mountains above us, and saw the trellised bridges between peaks, the rail track disappearing into tunnels cut half way up the side of a mountain. It is an extraordinary engineering feat, which took over forty years to complete.

Until they could bring in enough business, the passenger service would only run once a month. I told friends I was getting tickets and asked if they wanted to come, but there were unusual amounts of weddings going on that weekend and they had invitations. Nicky and I had our hearts set, so we decided to go ahead. The altitude alone should have put me off the trip, but it didn't. I felt that during the twelve hour trip up we would have more than enough time to acclimate.

Our taxi picked us up before dawn and drove us through the centre of Lima. The city was peaceful at that hour, with only a few cars on the road. We raced down the narrow streets lined with colonial buildings; their wooden balconies cantilevered over the sidewalk, and latticed to allow noblewomen to look out on the world without being seen by the public. All the neglect and decay of this great heritage was now hidden by the muted light. We emerged into the Plaza de Armas and just behind the Presidential Palace we saw the station. The sun was coming up, but it was still cold as we waited outside with the rest of the passengers.

Vendors walked up and down the queue, selling chicle, toilet paper, and bottles of water, which we bought out of boredom or for "the just in case" situations. After waiting for some time an official came to tell us: "Sorry we're late, but not enough passengers have booked, and we've had to arrange extra cargo to offset some of the expense of the trip." I thought it hardly mattered to add a couple more hours to a twelve hour trip, and better for us to have fewer people on the train.

It wasn't until we got on board that I discovered the degree of discomfort we were going to have to endure for the next fourteen hours. The seats were hard and upright like pews, with no padding to speak of. Under the narrow table between our seats my knees were pressing up against the English couple sitting opposite us. There was hardly any space at all, either for us or for our luggage, but by the time we discovered this we were already on board and psyched up to go.

We were a motley group of travellers: Americans, English, a few students from Europe, a couple of Peruvians, and two German photographers who had come to document the trip. It wasn't luxurious or expensive, but the trip was an interesting diversion for people with time on their hands and who were curious to do something outside the usual tourist agenda. The train also provided an alternative to people who were afraid of driving to Huancayo, the mountain roads are notoriously dangerous.

We left more or less on time, only about an hour late, and it was then that we were introduced to the cabin nurse who had been walking through the carriages wearing a crisp white uniform. We were told she was there to help us during the trip. I thought having a nurse on board was a bit excessive, but I quickly put her out of my mind. There were other things to think about, especially when after an hour we ended up back at the same station from where we left. I asked the couple opposite me: "Isn't that the same station?" They nodded: "It certainly looks like it, and it has the same name." We joked: "This is part of the adventure of travel, the unpredictable circumstances, the worst trips provide the best stories to take home."

The representatives came on board to explain: "We've picked up the cargo we told you about, and now that everything is loaded you are on your way." So far everyone was optimistic. A couple of hours late wasn't too bad. But that wasn't to be the case, nor was this to be our only stop. There would be many more to come.

Shortly after, we came to a halt because the engine malfunctioned, and at the next station we stopped and changed to a more powerful engine. Ours couldn't support the extra weight from the cargo. After that, I quit counting the stops. But I was grateful they were sorting out the problems now rather than when we were miles away from all the stations, or worse, stuck inside of one of the tunnels.

Nicky was playing quietly with a boy a few seats away, so I talked with the English couple opposite me. This was their annual trip abroad, which they meticulously planned all year, and they never stopped taking photos. They spread their mass of maps and guide-books across the table, inviting me to take a look. I confessed: "I know nothing about the train or Huancayo, other than what I read in the advertisement."

They told me: "Henry Meiggs, a compatriot of yours, built the railroad. He was a brilliant man who got caught in the property boom, and he ended up in South America after selling forged warrants and issuing unauthorized stock to cover a property deal in California that went bust. He escaped to South America on one of his own ships before the fraud was discovered, taking his family into exile. Eventually he paid back all his debts, but he never returned to the United States."

Meiggs began his career in South America building railroads in Chile, and after a few years he gained a reputation as being one of the best. In 1868 he moved to Peru, during the time of President Balta, who was keen to modernize the country by building railroads and connecting Peru's natural resources to the market place. Balta speculated that the railroads would bolster the economy and be a huge financial success. However, millions had to be borrowed from foreign lenders in order to build them, and that debt, along with the war against Chile, brought Peru to the verge of bankruptcy. Many of Meiggs' railroads are still in use today; his innovations and high standards are legendary. He was also known for paying his workers proper wages and for looking after them, long before the laws came in to protect them.

From the very start our trip was beset with problems. It seemed as if we were carrying as many mechanics as passengers, and every time we stopped because of the latest glitch they flooded outside for another inspection. It wasn't long before we went through our first tunnel, and it was then that we realized that none of the cabin lights worked. Every time we went through a tunnel we were plunged into darkness, and remained so until the train emerged at the other end. Sometimes one of the technicians would shine his flashlight down the aisle to provide us with light, but they soon lost interest, so we were left to fumble around in the dark as best we could. We were all praying the lights would be fixed, although no one was optimistic. Otherwise we would have to spend the last half of the trip without light, and none of us could imagine how we could cope in complete darkness for hours on end.

From the start, the train felt more like riding a ship in a storm. We pitched back and forth, rocking from side to side as we made our way up. At first we laughed and enjoyed the novelty, but by the time we had climbed to nearly sixteen thousand feet and I could hardly breathe I started to feel more like a prisoner on the train trip to hell.

I commented on our situation to the couple opposite me: "I wonder what strange character flaw we must possess to be sitting on this train for hour after hour and slowly suffocating. If we had any sense we would organize a mutiny and force the train to descend."

Our carriage looked more like a hospital car than a journey for pleasure. People were doing their best to lie down, depending on space. Only the students were thoroughly enjoying themselves. They were jumping up and down, taking photos of each other and playing cards. They were also drinking beer and eating peanuts, the smell from which kept wafting in our direction. But it was comforting to have people around who weren't sick.

Nicky started feeling ill from so much running around, and he asked me to take him to the loo, which was outside, between carriages. As we left our cabin the train jolted, throwing us against the wall. At the same time one of the doors to the outside swung open, slamming into the wall next to us. I dreaded to think that Nicky had been out there earlier playing with another child. Not only did the exit door not lock while the train was in motion, but the door itself didn't close properly. I held onto the window and swung it shut, before we made our way into the filthy loo.

Near the highest point of the trip Nicky felt worse, his breathing became shallow and he begged: "Mummy help me, my head is going to explode." He looked dreadful. His eyes were dark and sunken. I felt like the worst mother in the world for bringing him on the trip; and there were still hours to go.

Nicky lay down on our narrow bench while I perched on the edge, stroking his back and speaking softly to him, trying to help him relax and fall asleep, but he was in too much pain. The nurse came over and recommended giving him oxygen, and she sent her assistant running off to get it. I was horrified that she put the mask over his face without cleaning it first and that one of the tanks she brought was already empty. The oxygen went from person to person, and when it ran out we were out of luck.

Nicky eventually fell asleep, and one of the people sitting opposite gave me their seat so that I could sit more comfortably and keep an eye on him. I was trying hard to keep myself from being sick, and a bit later when the nurse came back to check on Nicky she brought me a tablet for nausea and a cup of water. When I swallowed the water, I gagged. It had a strong metallic taste. I asked: "Where did you get this water?" She shrugged her shoulders and told me: "From the train." I could tell it wasn't from a bottle by the taste. I also dreaded to think about how many other people had already shared the same cup. After drinking the water, I felt worse. I knew I couldn't make it to the loo in time, so I put my head under the table and started vomiting into a plastic bag.

Normally I would have been mortified to be vomiting next to strangers, but they pretended not to notice. I heaved until there was nothing left. Then I carefully knotted my sick bag, secured it under the bench, and fell asleep. I drifted off to that glorious place where pain and suffering are momentarily suspended when I was thrown violently against the edge of the table and abruptly brought back to my senses. Music blasted out over the speakers to distract

231

us from whatever new problem had arisen. When a maintenance man came through our carriage I grabbed his jacket with both hands and told him: "Turn down the music!" He said: "Señora, you don't like the music?" I said: "No! My son is ill, and don't you dare wake him." Then the first miracle of the trip happened, and there was complete silence.

I took advantage of the motionless train and dragged myself over to our guide and gave our return tickets away. I couldn't bear to have the dreaded things in my pocket any longer. We met the guide while he was handing out brochures in the station. He signed us up with some others for a couple of market tours outside Huancayo. When I gave him our tickets he realized how ill I had become and he put our tours on hold. Then he called ahead and arranged for a car to meet us at the station. That was our saving grace. By the time the train arrived in Huancayo, it was so late that the local cabs had given up waiting and gone home, only the few cars that were reserved were still there. He also helped by taking our bags off the train, and carried them to the car for us. As we were leaving the station Nicky patted me on the arm and said, "Mummy, thank you for taking me to Huancayo, but please could we never come again?" We both managed to laugh for the first time in hours.

When we arrived at the hotel, the porter took us straight to our room. The receptionist saw I was in no condition to fill out forms, so she only asked to see our passports. Nicky got into his pyjamas and I got ready for bed, but just the effort of brushing my teeth made me sick again. To further add to my misery, there was a wedding celebration going on in the courtyard below our window. At times the music was so loud that it felt as if the party had joined us in our room. I tossed and turned in my cold damp bed with a lumpy pillow and eventually fell into a restless sleep.

Nicky woke early and told me: "Mummy, I'm hungry. Come on, wake up, let's see what they're serving for breakfast." He hadn't eaten since lunch the previous day; so we got dressed, and headed down to find something to eat. There was a huge buffet in the dining room, laid across three tables. Nicky was famished and wanted to try everything. All I wanted was black tea and toast, and I wasn't sure if even that was a good idea.

While Nicky was deciding on what to eat, an American couple came over and asked me if we had come up on the train. They were in the next carriage and recognized us. We started talking and I invited them to join us for breakfast. They told me that they had also given their return tickets away. The woman described the journey as, "The train trip to hell". I told her: "Those were my words, verbatim." They had hired a car and driver to take them back to Lima the following day and they invited us to join them. I said: "No thank you, we are leaving Huancayo as soon as I can find a bus."

I wasn't feeling well, and I wanted to get home. Plus it was safer using one of the bus companies, which were regulated, than a car and driver whom we knew nothing about. There was also a teachers' strike going on in Peru, and the strikers had been illegally blocking some of the roads back to Lima. I wanted to get home before the problem escalated. We booked tickets on the earliest bus to avoid driving through the mountains at night. The route back to Lima goes through Ticlio and uses the same road on which Peter and I had seen the terrible accident. We had no other choice, it was either drive or take the train, as there wasn't an airport in Huancayo. Nicky and I walked around town. We went into the main market looking for souvenirs, and then to the cathedral to light candles for a safe trip home.

The cab dropped us at the bus terminal, but the second he left I realized I had forgotten the boxed lunches the hotel had prepared for us. Our concierge advised me to bring food, as they didn't serve meals on the bus. I left Nicky in charge of the bags while I ran outside looking for a shop, but there was nothing except a small kiosk selling sandwiches and local pastries. Normally I wouldn't buy food from someone selling in the street but, as we were to be on a bus for five or six hours and because Nicky wouldn't have anything to eat, everyone would have shared their food with him, which was just as risky. When the seller saw me, she shooed the flies off with a grubby rag, to give me a better look. I bought bottled water and bananas, and everything I could find in factory sealed packages. Afterwards I accepted a few additional items in lieu of change, as she didn't have any yet.

The bus seemed like a dream after the train. Our velvet seats were soft, and they reclined. Such comfort was hard to imagine after the trip up. After admiring our seats, we looked around and realized that we were the only passengers seated in the front row. We were the only tourists. Everyone else was sitting further back, which seemed odd. I felt embarrassed; I thought we were being segregated.

There was a glass partition with a curtain separating the driver from the passengers, and on the door there was a large sign, written in several languages, stating that it was forbidden to disturb the driver while the bus was in motion. Everyone settled in for the long trip, but shortly after our departure an old woman sent someone forward to knock on the driver's door to ask him to stop at one of the food stands by the side of the road. She needed water in order to take her medicine. No one seemed annoyed by the inconvenience, including the driver, who was very accommodating. While we were stopped for her water some people got on, selling fruit and freshly baked bread. We set off again and hadn't gone far before someone else realized that they hadn't brought enough bananas to survive the trip, so we stopped again. Now everyone was happy.

A bit later, and just when we were on one of the roughest parts of the trip, with the tightest curves, Nicky told me he needed to go to the loo, and he asked me to take him. I said: "No, you're well enough to go on your own." But he persisted until I agreed to take him. We held on for dear life as we made our way to the back of the bus, and when I opened the door of the loo I realized it had been a good idea for me to come with him. At least, I could keep him from getting hurt, and also so he didn't, God forbid, touch anything. We were both being tossed around because of the curves, and the next thing I knew we hit the bathroom door with such force that we broke the lock, and both of us went flying out of the door together. From the ground we saw startled faces peering down at us, but after they realized that we were okay they turned back and continued watching the film.

I couldn't move. I thought my leg was broken. Nicky was okay, he was laughing. I was so grateful he wasn't hurt that I laughed with him. There we were, sprawled across the floor with my feet still in the loo where I had left them. We were wedged between the seats, and I couldn't get up until a man took pity on us and grabbed me by the arm, determined he pulled me to my feet. Just as we stood up, the three of us were thrown across the aisle onto the lap of another man who was seated next to the loo, and then onto another man on the other side of the bus. I felt like a loose cannon.

By now I needed to use the loo. After thanking everyone Nicky went back to his seat, and I went back in the loo, hoping the door would stay shut and that I wouldn't be thrown out, this time with my pants down. One of the men watching from the back of the bus signalled me that he would hold the door closed with his foot, but we both knew he wouldn't be able to keep it shut if I was thrown against it again.

When Nicky and I returned to Lima, a couple friends came over to hear about our trip. They laughed at the miserable parts. They told me: "It's a pity! You should have stayed here. You missed a fabulous wedding." When I showed them my bruises they said: "You are lucky not to have been bouncing around on the bus with a broken leg. The driver wouldn't have been able to stop for you, and I doubt they carry anything for pain."

They were also shocked to hear that we had sat in the front of the bus. They told me: "Are you crazy to sit in the front with Nicky? That is the most dangerous place. The people in front are always the first to die in an accident. Only tourists are stupid enough to sit there. You ought to have known better."

I emailed my cousin Richard in London: "Dispatches from the train," telling him about our dismal trip up. I was surprised when he wrote back that he had taken the same train in the 1970s. He wrote: "It was not too nice in the train, which was crowded and smelly, so I opened the door at the end of the car and sat on the step in the fresh air with my legs dangling, to watch the view passing. Boys on the side of the track threw buckets of water over me as we passed them and then the temperature started falling and I got very cold indeed. It was not a very happy experience, but at least I did not get sick."

THE BIG EARTHQUAKE

Giannina arrived early and we talked while I was rushing to get ready. Naguib had invited us to a talk he was giving on his book of parables and paintings, and I didn't want to be late. Nicky was in my room begging me to let him come. We had houseguests from London, Oliver and Stefano, who were also coming, but because it was a school night Nicky had to stay home. He kept arguing: "Mummy, it's educational. I've finished my homework. Everyone else is going. Naguib is my friend too. He gave me a copy of his book. He will want me to be there. You can't leave me at home."

I was putting on my shoes and trying to change the subject when the building gave its first almighty shake. Normally tremors last only a few seconds, but as soon as the building began shaking, Giannina leapt across the room and crouched in the fetal position against the wall screaming: "Muffi, this is the end of the world." I told her: "No, come on Giannina, we're okay, it will stop any second. It only feels strong because we are on the seventh floor. You feel it more the higher up you get."

Oliver and Stefano ran to my bedroom, followed by Irma. Oliver was wrapped in a towel. He had been in the shower when the tremor started. Stefano was already dressed. I was squatting down hugging Giannina and running back to my desk trying to protect my computer and all my little treasures that were falling off and scattering in all directions. Normally Nicky hated earthquakes, they were our biggest dread while living in Peru, but this time he burst out laughing. The situation was comical in a sense, with Oliver wrapped in a towel beside Stefano, both wide eyed and wondering what to do, next to Giannina who was on the floor crying: "We're going to die." Irma stayed silent.

Nicky's laughter brought me to my senses. His reaction was unexpected and so out of character for him. I shouted over the noise: "Nicky stop! It's not funny. You've been through this before and they haven't, they're frightened." However, secretly I was grateful he wasn't afraid. It would have been impossible for me to take Nicky out and leave without Giannina, and she wouldn't move. He told me, "Mummy, it's my nervous laugh, I can't help it." I said: "Yes you can, and now is as good a time as any to start."

Our guests were in the doorway hoping for instructions when suddenly the building gave another massive shake. Giannina crossed herself and began screaming, "This is it, we are going to die. Muffi this is the end of the world!" And the boys ran for their lives, probably thinking 'She's Peruvian, so she would know about earthquakes,' and they bolted out of the room. It is not always safe to evacuate during an earthquake. People have run from their apartments and have been knocked over and trampled by others panicking to escape, others have fallen down steps. I shouted from the bedroom: "Don't take the lift." Afterward I turned to her and said, "Giannina, calm down for goodness sake! You are going to have a heart attack!" and I offered her a whiskey. Which she still teases me about today. She tells me: "I thought we were going to die and you offered me a whiskey. You frightened me more because I thought you had lost your mind."

The tremor went on and on, seeming to get worse, rising and subsiding in waves. But there was nothing we could do. Nicky and I had been through earthquakes before, though not as strong as this one, so we knew the building was strong. However, when it didn't stop, I lost confidence that any building could continue to withstand a pounding at this strength. Nicky threw his voice above the noise and asked, "Mummy, if you're still going to go to Naguib's talk, may I come with you? You can't leave me alone with Irma after an earthquake, it wouldn't be safe." A bit later he asked, "Mummy, will I have to go to school tomorrow?" I shouted back: "Nicky for heaven's sake shut up, we'll talk about it later."

It was difficult to walk. The floor was moving, disorientating me as it shuffled us around with the furniture. The windows were banging together, sounding as if at any moment they would shatter. I kept running back to Giannina, hugging her and then running out to check for cracks, keeping light on my feet, worried that at any second the floor would break open and swallow us up. The tremor lasted almost three minutes, and when it was over Irma automatically went around and started cleaning up the breakage. I told her: "Please get out. Go down in case it starts again." So she picked up Spot and left.

I have read that animals can sense an earthquake coming, and they become agitated, even hours or days before the earthquake begins. But not Spot. He had been floundering around on the wooden floor like a beached whale, and he wasn't in the slightest bit nervous or edgy. I think he quite enjoyed it.

The phone rang. It was Hugh telling me that he wasn't coming to collect us. He told me: "Muffi, the talk will be cancelled, and, besides, we wouldn't be able to get through the traffic to reach the centre of Lima. Everywhere will be in chaos."

I had been looking forward to the evening, and I said, "Oh come on Hugh, let's go. It will be fun and, besides, we're ready."

He asked, "Are you mad? No one is going there, after an earthquake people will stay home. The lecture will be cancelled, but come here if you want. You'll be safer in my house where you can get out quickly if it starts up again. There will be hundreds of aftershocks following an earthquake like this."

By the time I got off the phone Giannina had left. She hadn't said goodbye and I wasn't sure if she was in a safe state to drive. I couldn't get through to her by phone. Everyone had left the apartment by then. I changed out of my high heels and evening clothes into jeans and took a bottle of single malt whiskey from my closet, a gift saved for a special occasion. I thought everyone would want a drink, so I stopped in the kitchen and searched for plastic cups. My keys were in my pocket. I patted my jacket several times to double check. I worried that everyone in their haste to leave would have forgotten their keys, and if I forgot mine we would need a locksmith to get back in. Keys and whiskey became my mantra; we would never have found a locksmith who would come out tonight.

I was the only one left in the apartment, and I suddenly felt like dancing. I felt strangely elated and found it hard to keep from laughing. I thought, "Oh my God that was unbelievable. Did you see the looks on their faces? What an extraordinary experience to survive. What a dinner party conversation; a frisson of fear, an adrenaline rush - maybe I have found my thrill."

I walked over to the window and looked down at the blanket of people scrambling around in the street below. I felt all-powerful and unafraid. Me: The goddess of the mountain looking down upon her subjects, reigning triumphantly. I savored the moment. Running on pure adrenaline, I swirled around the room, punching the air in a victory salute. I said, "Daddy, Grandpa, did you see that, did you see me? I was utterly amazing."

However, seconds later, as I descended the steps I regained my senses. It was common knowledge, living in a seismic zone, "Never take the lift during an earthquake." But I had also read that the stairs, our only other means of escape, vibrate at a different moment of frequency than the building during an earthquake, thereby weakening them; so theoretically, they probably weren't safe. Our concrete steps, which were external and open on the sides like a fire escape, had vibrated at a different moment of frequency for what felt like an eternity, and so it was with a pounding heart and wobbly legs that I continued my descent. I wracked my brain to remember what I was told. Was I supposed to wait in the flat to be rescued, or wait until someone came to tell me the stairs were safe? My mind was blank. Seven flights down, and with each and every agonising step I imagined the stairway giving way, crumbling, disintegrating beneath my feet, and my body freefalling into space; a flash of unbearable pain and then death. Was Nicky in the crowd? Was he watching? "Please God protect me."

The Porter was still inside, waiting by his desk. Marble panels had broken loose from the walls and shattered across the floor in the entrance, and it looked as if a bomb had exploded. He helped me out over the rubble, through the garage and into the street. All the residents of the surrounding houses and buildings were outside, frightened and cut off from the security and comfort of their homes. The street was full of people shoulder-to-shoulder, stranded together. I saw terrified nannies with young mothers holding babies bundled in blankets, children clinging to their families, elderly people in wheelchairs, nurses and porters; everyone was in the street, waiting. People huddled in groups, talking or trying to get through on their phones, all of us wondering, what next? Catastrophes create solidarity. Some men were trying to create order, shouting: "Get away from the buildings and out from under the power lines. Run to the park where it is safe." However few of us were taking any notice. Mostly people were vigilantly keeping their families together or had their ears glued to a cellular phone.

None of my neighbours wanted the whiskey I offered. They politely refused. I took a large shot of the whiskey and savored its smooth warm glorious taste, so did Oliver and Stefano. They were thrilled I had thought to bring whiskey. "Medicinal," we proclaimed to the odd gawker, as we continued passing the bottle between us. Nicky and Irma were talking with the security guards behind our building, and, after exchanging a few animated earthquake experiences with some of the neighbours, we headed off to Hugh's.

There were several accidents in the street; distracted drivers rear-ended each other when the road heaved and people came flooding out of buildings from all directions. No one was injured, but they left their cars blocking the road. A great carpet of humanity trailed down the street, most of them redialing cellular phones, trying to get through to family and friends. We wove in and out through the crowd, walking single file, with Spot and Irma leading followed by Nicky, Oliver, Stefano, and myself. After a few blocks and several whiskeys later, I was relaxed. The air pinged with excitement, crowds in the street made it feel like a carnival. We had survived the earthquake. This was cause for celebration. I felt like hugging people in the street.

Mari, Hugh's maid, opened the door when we arrived. She hadn't recovered from the earthquake, and was looking worse after seeing the arrival of so many of Hugh's guests. Hugh shot past as we were coming in and told us: "I'm going to check on my daughters. I haven't been able get through to them on the phone." He told us: "Wait here or come with me and I will drop you back at your apartment. You'll need some extra pillows and blankets if you want to stay tonight." We piled into the car with Hugh and he dropped us back at our building and sped away.

We felt the aftershocks as we headed up in the lift. They were much stronger than I had expected. I dashed around the apartment gathering clothes, blankets, my computer and Spot's food. It felt like being in a game of musical chairs, each of us vying to be closest to the door and first out in case the earthquake started again. The entry phone buzzed and I ignored it; we weren't expecting guests. I thought it was the Porter checking on us. But when Nicky heard the buzzer, he called the lift and Ricardo, the brother of Mercedes, Peter's first wife, stepped into the room. He had just arrived at his hotel when the earthquake started. The huge television in his bedroom had shaken itself off the ledge and crashed to the floor, shattering in a puff of smoke, and while maintenance was in clearing up the mess, he drove over to check on us.

I told him about Giannina, and that we were staying the night with Hugh. He offered to drive us back to Hugh's, but he agreed that first I should check on Giannina. We piled into his car with Nicky, Oliver, Stephen, plus pillows, blankets, laptops and luggage, and headed off to see if Giannina was all right. We couldn't reach her by phone. Everyone in Lima was trying to get through to someone, which had overwhelmed the phone system.

Giannina's district was without power, nor were there lights in the street. I didn't recognize where we were. Ricardo didn't know where she lived and we went around in circles trying to find her house. We saw people outside, huddled in groups, probably afraid to go back inside. Without light it would be more difficult to get out if there was another earthquake. Rumors circulated that a much bigger earthquake was coming, which kept everyone on edge.

Giannina was outside the house, talking to her cook. She was preoccupied with dinner. Without power the cook couldn't prepare food, and her daughters wanted to eat. We were on our way to meet Hugh at a local restaurant, so we invited them to join us. Everyone piled back into the car, this time with Giannina, Maria

José, and Gianninita, plus Nicky, Stefano, Oliver, and me, together with our luggage. The car's undercarriage scraped the road on every bump. Our nerves were on edge, all of us praying that it could withstand our extra weight and that we wouldn't be left stranded in the street.

We found Hugh seated at a long wooden table, holding court with family and friends. All of them were laughing and reaching out in unison to rescue the bottles of wine dancing around the table from the aftershocks. Everyone shared animated earthquake stories, we laughed until our bodies ached. Several people were caught in the shower; one was having a bikini wax and ran from the salon half naked.

The euphoria would quickly fade but after experiencing the earthquake and fearing an untimely end, life with all of its vicissitudes and uncertainties looked good. An earthquake is a great reminder that nothing is permanent. In a flash, everything can change. There are no safety nets in life; no guarantees. After finishing my wine, I raised my glass to life and, God willing, many more adventures.

END

Printed in Great Britain
by Amazon

36258383R00145